Brand Romance

Brand Romance

Using the Power of High Design to Build a Lifelong Relationship with Your Audience

By Yasushi Kusume

and

Neil Gridley

First published 2013 by
PALGRAVE MACMILLAN

Palgrave Macmillan in the UK is an imprint of Macmillan Publishers Limited, registered in England, company number 785998, of Houndmills, Basingstoke, Hampshire RG21 6XS.

Palgrave Macmillan in the US is a division of St Martin's Press LLC, 175 Fifth Avenue, New York, NY 10010.

Palgrave Macmillan is the global academic imprint of the above companies and has companies and representatives throughout the world.

Palgrave® and Macmillan® are registered trademarks in the United States, the United Kingdom, Europe and other countries.

ISBN: 978–1–137–36900–0 hardback

This book is printed on paper suitable for recycling and made from fully managed and sustained forest sources. Logging, pulping and manufacturing processes are expected to conform to the environmental regulations of the country of origin.

A catalogue record for this book is available from the British Library.

A catalog record for this book is available from the Library of Congress.

This book is dedicated to Stefano Marzano and his philosophy of High Design.

As a profession, design is still young. Yet it's built on a very old foundation: the core humanist values that, in different ways and in different modalities, have always helped people to progress along the path of civilization. In the coming century, we will face a number of important issues and designers, technologists and marketers – working in an equal partnership – will need to lead the way in working out how to bridge the gap between our current reality and the long-term ideals of civilization. They will need to help us create a better quality of life, and chart the path we need to take to get there. It is only such a long-term, planned approach that is most likely to ensure a sustainable future for us all.

Stefano Marzano, 1999

Contents

List of Figures

A Note to the Reader

There are many different brands, serving many different types of people. For some, the word *customer* is the most accurate description; for others *end-user*, or *consumer*, or even *client*. To avoid confusion, and to remove any doubts that we are writing for a specific industry or group of brands, we have decided to use the word *audience* to embrace all types.

Introduction

Much as two parents offer unconditional love to their children, a "loved" brand offers unconditional love to its specific audience. And just as with parents, such a brand should not expect any return of that love. Instead, if it treats its loved ones with true care and attention, then they will – we believe – come to understand the brand's values and beliefs. And when they come to share those values and beliefs, they will return the brand's love to it.

Love between people represents a choice and a long-term commitment. In much the same way, a brand can also choose to build a loving connection with its audience. When, as a brand owner and/or CEO of a company, you make such a choice, then the questions you have to face are:

- Do you really understand people's needs, experiences and feelings?

- How do you understand people and engage with them emotionally?

- How do you find a way not just to meet their needs, but to make them realize that that is what you are doing?

The aim of this book is to show how your brand can harness the power of design to build a "loving relationship" with your audience. It will describe how you can use design to construct an emotional engagement with your audience, and to take the lead over your company and brand by applying design thinking and capability.

It will tell you, in short, how to build a truly "loved brand" by design.

WHAT IS A BRAND?

Before we dive into design and the ways in which you can utilize its power to build a loving relationship with your audience, we would first like to clarify what we believe a brand is.

In his book *The Brand Gap*, Marty Neumeier stated that a brand isn't a logo, a product or a corporate identity. He wrote, "A brand is a person's gut feeling about a product service, or company. It's not what you say it is. It's what *they* say it is."

While we fully agree with this definition, we would go a step further and say that a brand is also what people feel it is. It is defined by people's instincts and "gut" decisions. In *Start with Why*, Simon Sinek (2009) describes where such "gut decisions" come from.

> There is no part of the stomach that controls decision-making, it all happens in the limbic brain. It's not an accident that we use that word "feel" to explain those decisions either. The reason gut decisions feel right is because the part of the brain that controls them also controls our feelings. Whether you defer to your gut or you're simply following your heart, no matter which part of the body you think is driving the decision, the reality is it's all in your limbic.

People's perceptions are subjective and selective. If your brand is defined by what people are *feeling*, then that perception is built from their subjective and selective emotions. And that is why design can play an important role for a brand, because its enduring role is to ensure that a brand makes the right emotional connection with its audience. By creating that emotional connection – by enabling a brand to build a trusted relationship with audiences, just as loving couples build trust with each other, design is building a "loved" brand.

in the world today, as we listen to the news, the quest for Paradise Regained may seem to be an impossible, unreachable illusion. Perhaps it is; perhaps it isn't. But if it guides us in making the right choices, if it inspires us to learn the things we need to know to do good with our design, it will serve its purpose. In the final analysis, design is an act of love.

Stefano Marzano,
Philips Design annual event 2005

A LOVED BRAND

The best way to illustrate how a "loved" brand works is to ask you to think about how you built a loving relationship with you own partner.

First sight

Do you remember the first time you saw them? Before you actually *met* them? They very probably made some impression on you with their appearance. Perhaps it was their face, or another part of their body, or even what they were wearing that day. It might have happened in an instant or gradually, over time. But however it happened, it almost certainly started with (some part of) their appearance.

We believe that exactly the same idea applies to a brand and a brand proposition. And it explains why a brand should apply design thinking and capability to give it a striking appearance – an appearance that not only makes it irresistible to those who encounter it, but also one that forces them to engage fully with each and every one of its touchpoints.

Getting to know them

So, having met someone whose appearance attracted you, you found a way to approach them. And from there a deeper, more emotional bond began to grow – adding a more intense level of attraction by experiencing the way they smiled at your jokes, the way they talked or just their body language. It's exactly the same for a brand: a brand and its proposition should try to build an emotional bond with its audience. To put it another way, a product should be designed with qualities that engage the audience's relevant senses, to give it qualities that continuously surprise, delight and differentiate it from other brands.

A real partner

Finally, after you'd spent time together, you began to discover your partner's character and personality and, from there, to touch on their values and beliefs. Then, when you realized that you shared most – or all – of those values and beliefs you recognized that you had found a real partner, someone with whom you could build a truly loving relationship. It's just such a connection that a brand and a proposition should try to achieve with its audience. And to do that, design thinking and capability needs to be totally honest about what the brand is and what its beliefs are.

The key

What we are trying to pinpoint here is the key to building a true love: the discovery, and sharing, of each other's values and beliefs. And while this may begin with appearance, that appearance is not – unless you're just looking for a "one night stand" – the ultimate key to success. So it is with a brand: it may look good, but unless it shares its audience's values and beliefs, there will be no true love between the two.

THE MEANING OF LOVE

Before we go any further, it's important to note that we are not using the word "love" in just its spiritual and metaphoric sense. In the context of brands and audiences, "love" has two very specific aspects.

One is a natural desire to deeply understand and embrace those you love – and not just their positive but also their negative sides. You want to be the one who best understands *all* their mental and physical aspects, everything from values, motivations, needs, desires, hopes and dreams to problems, worries, jealousies, hatreds and fears.

The other is the satisfaction of your loved one. Do you only think about their short-term pleasure, or do you also try to anticipate their long-term happiness. Are you the one who best understands what they really want and need?

If the answer is yes, then you've built a truly loving relationship with your audience. The question then is: how do you go about building that love?

In any relationship, a positive first impression is critical. But as time goes on and the relationship develops, it is important that consecutive experiences and interactions confirm those original positive first impressions. This also applies to brands and end-users for which the brand acts as a trust portal. People who are prepared to commit themselves to a brand are looking for integrity, confidence and authenticity and design plays a very important role in building this. Design is able to create a series of experiences that increase satisfaction, bonding and loyalty, as in any other fulfilling relationship. Design helps identify what is at the core of a company, differentiating and enhancing it by providing appropriate propositions across all touchpoints of the brand. As designers we continually explore how each moment contributes to the user's experience of the brand, how it will influence their relationship with it and what we can do to further build and develop our relationship with them.

This relationship – an experience-based romance – guides what should be our fundamental question as designers and as a brand: Does your customer love you?

Stefano Marzano, 2011

Markets are becoming more competitive every day. More than 20 years in the business have shown us that people have started to solely rely on rational aspects to make business decisions. We believe this is a negative phenomenon of a very competitive environment. We see that people rely on rational measures (something you can measure with numbers) and data because these are linked to being perceived as "true professional". But in people's every day personal lives, they balance rational and emotional value to make a correct "decision" that feels right. Nobody tries to fill in a spreadsheet of ROI (return on investment) when they are out with their loved one. Nobody asks ROI of love in their personal life! This book will remind us what we have forgotten about and give us a structured way of achieving it.

We consider the answer to how to build a truly loving relationship with your audience to be High Design.

A HIGHER FORM OF DESIGN

Before we translate High Design into more detail, we think it's a good idea to touch on precisely what we mean by "design".

Stefano Marzano, the man to whom this book is dedicated, calls it Design – with a capital D – and sees it as a higher form of design, something more than just product styling, aesthetics or graphical execution. For him, Design can and must be concerned with a broader picture, one that includes brand, business, technology, customers and the end-user context.

To be truly effective, it must offer relevant and meaningful solutions that satisfy people's needs, empower them and make them happier. At the same time, it must contribute to the stakeholder's prosperity and, above all, respect the world we live in. It must treat customers with love and create direct, holistic brand experiences for all.

It must be "High" Design.

HIGH DESIGN

Stefano Marzano introduced the concept of High Design in 1991 in *Flying over Las Vegas*, but let us refer to the origin of his thinking of High Design from his early speech "Creative Culture". He said:

> During the XV century the word "humanism" was associated with the intellectual "summa". For them the idea to embrace humanism and ignore the scientific and technological developments would have been incomprehensible!! I believe the same, and this is what has also inspired my vision of the "High Design" in 1991, however I think it is time to push it further, it is time to re-establish a new "Holism", to contribute to the new creative culture, to a new Humanism to drive the epoch toward a sustainable preferable future!

(Complexity = design, Hi complexity = Hi design,
Holistic complexity = Holistic Hi Design.)

The role of the humanist was the one to create a bridge
between the present and the future without losing
touch with the past. This role has now to be enriched
by a revival of the productive and creative thought for
the comprehension of the nature of the humankind.
The understanding of the reality of the physical, bio-
logical world and of the humanity that is capable to
take the best from physic, genetic, bio chemic, from
the research on the evolutionary theories and from
anthropology and philosophy. In search of new exper-
imental and empirical bases for more solid conclu-
sions about the "good" and the future.

Stefano Marzano wrote that the answer to dealing with
several layers of complexity in both the outside (i.e. society)
and the inside (i.e. organization) world may be sought in
what he called High Design.

By High Design, I mean an integrated process incorporating all the skills on which design has historically
based itself, plus all the new design-related skills we
need to be able to respond to the complexity and to
adopt more advanced cultural and technical criteria. It's
based on the fusion and interaction of high-level skills.
...
Design in a world of high complexity should no longer
be a case of clever individuals or teams creating products in splendid isolation, but of multidisciplinary
organisations or networks creating "relevant qualities" and "cultural spheres". If we're to make the
quantum leap from the limited materialistic and
quantitative market to the unlimited, more spiritual
and qualitative market, then we must provide the
design worthy of it.

Within this context, he claimed there are four important principles in High Design. It must be:

- People focused
- Business integrated
- Research based
- Multidisciplinary

HIGH DESIGN IS PEOPLE FOCUSED

> Everything that I understand, I understand
> only because I love.
> *Count Leo Tolstoy*

Nearly everything that is designed is designed for people, in one way or another. The man-made world around us has, for the most part, been developed on a human scale for people to interact with. Therefore if we are to truly approach design from a people-centred – or maybe it's better to say an outside-in (not inside-out) – perspective, we must focus fully on people to understand their future wants and current needs.

HIGH DESIGN IS BUSINESS INTEGRATED

> The limits of my language are the limits of
> my mind. All I know is what I have words
> for.
> *Ludwig Wittgenstein*

To maximize the value of design (thinking and capability) to achieve brand and business successes and growth, it is important to seamlessly integrate Design into both the brand strategy and the business process, *and* to maximize the collaboration with other functions.

HIGH DESIGN IS RESEARCH BASED

> I am the wisest man alive, for I know one
> thing, and that is that I know nothing.
> *Socrates*

It is vitally important to install a design process, and methods, that provide you with a way of accessing and working with your audience to co-create relevant and meaningful solutions. This process must be integrated into your normal ways of working and iterative so that solutions are evolved appropriately.

HIGH DESIGN IS MULTIDISCIPLINARY

> The minute we become an integrated
> whole, we look through the same eyes and
> we see a whole different world together.
> *Azizah Al-Hibri*

Design is all about people. It is Design's unique skill to be able to articulate and translate intangible foresights, insights and ideas into something tangible and "discussable" to all stakeholders. It is, in fact, a fundamental enabler for achieving true collaboration with all stakeholders (both inside and outside).

15 COMMITMENTS TO BUILD A LOVED BRAND

We, the authors, are both enthusiasts for, and strong believers in, the principles of High Design. By applying its philosophy to our day-to-day work for more than 20 years, we have come to realize that it provides the principles needed to build a truly "loved brand". So what follows – and is explored and translated in greater detail in the corresponding chapters of this book – are descriptions of the 15 "commitments" needed to build a loved brand. We've grouped them into four separate topics:

- Know who you are
- Know your audience
- Know what you will bring your audience
- Know how you will bring it to your audience

Know who you are

Commitment 1: Think of your brand as a person
A brand is just like a person, with values and beliefs that manifest themselves as personality, character and behaviours. This chapter describes how to structure your brand design by making it reflect human psychology.

Know your audience

Commitment 2: Understand short- and long-term needs
If you truly love your audience, you will not only think about its short-term satisfaction, but also anticipate its long-term happiness. This chapter describes the importance of understanding people from two perspectives: short-term and long-term needs – both tangible and latent.

Commitment 3: Co-create with people
"Co-creation" demands the creation of "a permanent emotional engagement with your audience". It does not mean involving people in only one phase of your business or

product creation process. This chapter describes the power of emotionally engaging your users and customers.

Commitment 4: Understand how people experience

An experience is personal, memorable and involving. This chapter describes the five stages of experience – imagination, impression, discovery, use and memory – and how to make the best use of them for a properly people-focused approach.

Commitment 5: Measure and optimize

When you organize design tests you must ask questions relevant to the needs of your audience. This chapter describes how to conduct long-term, effective design tests.

Commitment 6: Introduce a "love tester"

If you want to evaluate design performance and contribution fully, you need clear performance measurements. This chapter describes two design performance measurements we have used in our work.

Know *what* you will bring your audience

Commitment 7: Build a clear brand design architecture

You need a clear Brand Design Architecture to help you find a balance between the extension of a product range (leveraging your strong brand) and the maintenance of a strong brand image and associations. This chapter describes how to build such architecture by introducing higher-level propositions.

Commitment 8: Continuously innovate

If your brand is to maintain its long-term sustainability, it needs to continuously innovate. This chapter describes the challenges that innovation presents a brand and a company.

Commitment 9: Give your value proposition the four design drivers

Although it is extremely important for you to manage your brand portfolio carefully, it is just as important that you maximize the value of its focused propositions by strategically planning their scope. This chapter describes the four design drivers you can use to maximize the value of your propositions.

Know *how* you will bring it to your audience

Commitment 10: Create a clearly recognizable identity

A brand uses touchpoints to create a specific identity and differentiate itself from others. This chapter describes how you can create a recognizable design identity.

Commitment 11: Embrace the three design principles

If you truly love and care about others, you will want to fulfil their desires. This chapter describes three principles that contain simple, focused activities to help you uncover and fulfil the needs of your audience.

Commitment 12: Create one vocabulary for the whole organization

Communicating only by words has limitations when describing your plan – especially when using adjectives to describe its emotional aspects. This chapter describes how design works as an integrator, using its skills to translate topics into tangible forms through each stage of the business creation process.

Commitment 13: Recognize the maestro and the virtuoso

It is important to identify and install the two core leadership roles essential for the effective orchestration of a brand experience by the design function. This chapter describes the roles of maestro (conductor/orchestrator) and virtuoso (specialist).

Commitment 14: Nurture your talent

The one and only asset of design is people. This chapter describes how to install "open talent management" by focusing on the capability of what we call the "maestro".

Commitment 15: Create a shared culture

Building the right culture is vitally important. This chapter describes how the power of one shared culture extends far beyond the setting of policy, guidelines, KPIs (key performance indicators) and balanced score cards.

Part 1
Know Who You Are

1

Commitment 1: Think of Your Brand as a Person

> Your beliefs become your thoughts. Your thoughts become your words. Your words become your actions. Your actions become your habits. Your habits become your values. Your values become your destiny.
>
> *Mahatma Gandhi*

Have you ever considered yourself as a brand? If you did, you might ask the following questions:

- What are your values and beliefs?

- Where do they come from?

- Are they specific to you, or do you share them with other family members?

- How do other people perceive your personality?

- Are you perceived the way you want to be?

- Does your behaviour match your values and beliefs?

- Do you behave according to the situations you find yourself in?

- Is your appearance a reflection of your true self?

When people talk about a brand's identity, the majority tend to limit its scope to no more than a logo design and layout templates. Yet in his book *Brand Leadership* David Aaker compares a brand to a person (in the chapter "Brand Identity"). And as we suggested in the Introduction – when you compare the steps required to build a truly loved brand to the steps you might go through in finding a partner – it's fair to accept that a brand closely resembles a human being: it has its own values and beliefs, and they manifest themselves in the brand's personality and behaviour.

If a brand is like a person, then a brand's identity must resemble a person's identity, which implies that it is much more than mere logos and templates. And if that is so, is it possible to go further by identifying the ingredients of a human identity and, by extension, those of a brand?

This chapter discusses what all this means for a brand. It also looks at how, if you want to build a truly loved brand with an emotional engagement with your audience, you must first understand yourself – so you can fully express your values and beliefs to your audience.

PERSONAL IDENTITY

First, we need to determine what constitutes a person's identity. For the purposes of this book, we'd like to use a simple four layer structure to describe it:

- Factual data
- Beliefs and values
- Personality and character
- Behaviour and appearance

Factual data

This is the basic factual information about any person – such as name, age, place of birth and so on.

Beliefs and values

Beliefs, according to the website Difference Between.net:

> are the convictions that we generally hold to be true, usually without actual proof or evidence. They are often, but not always connected to religion.
> ...
> Beliefs are basically assumptions that we make about the world and our values stem from those beliefs. Our values are things that we deem important and can include concepts like equality, honesty, education, effort, perseverance, loyalty, faithfulness, conservation of the environment and many, many other concepts.

This can be summarized as follows:

1. Beliefs are concepts that we hold to be true.

2. Beliefs may become religion, but not always.

3. Values are ideas that we hold to be important.

4. Values govern the way we behave, communicate and interact with others.

5. Beliefs and values determine our attitudes and opinions.

Personality and character

Personality, as defined by one business dictionary, is a "relatively stable, consistent, and distinctive set of mental and emotional characteristics a person exhibits when alone, or when interacting with people and his or her external environment."

Alex Lickerman however, in his article "Happiness in this World" (*Psychology Today*, 2011), noted that "We judge people funny, extroverted, energetic, optimistic, confident — as well as overly serious, lazy, negative, and shy."

We believe personality is something formed by one's values and beliefs and that it reflects (or perhaps we should say, manifests itself through) one's behaviour. As a result, a person will be judged by others to *be* the behaviour they demonstrate: funny, introverted, serious, energetic, pessimistic, confident and so on.

Behaviour and appearance

For the *Concise Oxford Dictionary of Current English*, behaviour is, "the manner of conducting oneself." We think it's fair to say that most of us modify our behaviour and appearance to match the context we find ourselves in. Consider, for example, how you would dress and behave at a funeral or a wedding.

We all know people who care about their appearance and behaviour and try to make a certain impression on others, just as we also know others who seem not to care at all. In either case though, since appearance and then behaviour govern the first impressions we make on others (as we suggested in the Introduction), then they will have a major influence on how others perceive us.

For us, appearance and behaviour very definitely reflect personality, and therefore values and beliefs. (This is examined further in Chapter 9.)

A BRAND'S IDENTITY

As already noted, when a company talks about a brand's identity, it very often only focuses on logos and templates.

It tends to treat a brand's beliefs and values, as well as its personality, as something separate from its identity. Yet if a brand can be granted the same four layers of identity as a person, the following observations can be offered.

Brand factual data

This is the factual information about a brand: its name (logo or wordmark), the company colour (if applicable), the year of its origin and so on.

Brand beliefs and values

Over the past ten years the Design Council in London has been running a programme to help UK companies harness the power of design. Included in this was a series of master classes, one of which was about branding: "The What, Why and How of Branding". This pointed out that you need to make your values distinctive by keeping them precise, because most companies draw their values from a similar list of ten values: integrity, openness/transparency, innovation/being first, responsibility, fairness, respect, empowerment/passion, flexibility, teamwork, pride/satisfaction (SDL/The Research Business International, 1999).

Let's look at just one of these values: innovation. It's a very common value ... but it's not specific enough. Why and how you are innovative? How are you different from anyone else? The key is that you have begun from a unique starting point.

In *The Corporate Brand*, Nicholas Ind noted that, "In small companies it is often the convictions and beliefs of the founder that define the values and consequently the culture of the organization." Since every company and brand was "small" when it started, we believe every company's values and beliefs are strongly rooted in their founder's values and beliefs – you might also say their "purpose" – for the strongest brands are often driven by a leader at the beginning who

is on a mission to make a "dent in the universe", they are
the starting point for all companies and brands. Therefore
it is important to capture, as precisely as possible, the beliefs
and values of your company at its starting point, since most
companies and brands often tend to use similar wordings
when describing themselves.

Brand beliefs and values quite often manifest themselves
in the brand promise of a company. A brand promise is a
clear, relevant, authentic commitment that a brand makes
to its employees, customers and end-users; one that makes
it easy for them to understand what the brand stands for.
Its prime purpose is to state what differentiates their products and services (from competitors) by offering superior
quality, value or a competitive edge.

Duane E. Knapp defines a brand promise as:

> the essence of the benefits (both functional and emo-
> tional) that current and potential customers can
> expect to receive from experiencing a brand's prod-
> ucts and services. The brand promise incorporates the
> consumer's point of view and is intended to reflect the
> heart, soul and spirit of the brand. It's intended as an
> internal directive, not as an advertising message,
> although it should drive an organization's activities
> and messages.
> ...
> The brand promise should serve as the "guiding star"
> for everything an organization does. Its primary pur-
> pose is to communicate clearly to every stakeholder
> associated with an organization (employees, agents,
> representatives, etc.) what the brand stands for. A
> promise acts as a compass reading for everyone con-
> nected with a brand and also as a constant reality
> check to evaluate an organization's activities, perfor-
> mance and priorities.
>
> Duane E. Knapp, *The Brand Mindset*, 2000

As already mentioned, Simon Sinek says it's the *"why"* that builds an emotional engagement with your brand, the sense of purpose that people can get behind and really believe in because, if it is based on your real values and convictions, it has authenticity. Often this is clear and raw with a start up company and as that company grows and takes on more staff this can get diluted, or even forgotten. Especially if the founder of the company moves on – as you grow up it is easy to creep away from why you decided to do what you do in the first place.

From 2001 to 2002, we were fortunate enough to be part of a team searching for the values of Philips. Philips was over 100 years old and the founder had long since left. The team began by investigating all the historical anecdotes they could find, as well as interviewing past and present employees. All the findings were then distilled into core messages designed to provide our internal stakeholders with the answers to several key questions:

- Where do we come from?

- What are we good at?

- How are we different?

- Who do we serve?

- How do we act?

- What do we believe in?

- Why do we do all this?

The answers to these questions then formed the company's Brand Foundation: the brand value and belief of the company strongly rooted in its founder's values and beliefs. This was the original sense of purpose which drove the founder to create a great business.

However one thing we noticed when we introduced this "foundation" was that people tended to take it as a new ideology and began asking for training and deployment in it. It was difficult for many of them to understand that what we were offering reflected not the way they should be but the way they actually were, that it was built upon the heritage and provenance of the company.

Company values and beliefs should be used as a confirmation of the company's promise, a promise that should not be compromised for financial gain or short-team business goals. That's why, if you are starting up a company, we would strongly suggest writing down your convictions and beliefs at the very beginning and offering them as your brand promise. If you are already in business, then you need to identify your values and beliefs so that the purpose of your actions will be totally clear to your internal stakeholders. And finally, it's important to note that, often, the challenge lies not in identifying your values and beliefs, but in helping internal stakeholders fully understand the need for having them in the first place.

Brand personality and character

In the same master class mentioned earlier – "The What, Why and How of Branding" – the Design Council describes a brand's personality as, "the way you express your values and give your company a human quality that customers can relate to." It's a tangible internal description designed to set and share how a brand "speaks" and "behaves". By personifying a brand, you can describe its emotional character and the associations about it that you want to generate in people's minds. You can provide a clear starting point for all your brand and company activities.

This is why we feel it would be both valuable and interesting to use the overview of personality offered by Cattell and Schuerger (2003) in their *Essentials of 16PF*

(*Personality Factor*) *Assessment.* The book describes 16 different fundamental components of personality: warmth, reasoning, emotional stability, dominance, liveliness, role consciousness, social boldness, sensitivity, vigilance, abstractedness, privateness, apprehension, openness to change, self-reliance, perfectionism and tension. Using these 16 components as a basis for internal company discussions would, we believe, help you to discuss and identify your brand personality.

BRAND BEHAVIOUR AND APPEARANCE

A brand's behaviour and appearance is essentially the interaction and visualization of your brand's touchpoints. For example, any advertising you see in a magazine, on a billboard, in a street or on retail packaging is all the appearance of a brand. You are exposed to hundreds of varieties of such appearances every day.

You also experience how brands behave by interacting with them daily. You may interact with them online, in retail environments or through products and services. Such interactions take place not only when people talk about them to others, but also when they deal with products, services and communications. (The UK bank First Direct has won many awards for its no-nonsense high quality and straightforward telephone banking service. When you deal with a member of a brand's service team, you associate the behaviour of that person with the brand.)

Although it might be obvious to you when you interact with a product such as a smart phone that you are experiencing brand behaviour, it is perhaps less obvious that when you use almost *any* product – for example, a TV – you are also experiencing that behaviour. On most brands of TV, the user doesn't just change the volume when they press the volume button on the remote: they also interact with the brand through that function. This is important because it's also possible for product, service or online communication interactions to operate in a way that manifests a company's attitude to its users. The way in which it uses such elements as light, sound and physical movements – and modifies their density, speed, strength, volume and duration – sends a specific behavioural message. It says something about the way the company sees its customers. And this is why the characteristics of the way an individual interacts with other individuals (their *behaviour*) can also be translated into the way products interact with individuals.

Therefore it is up to you how you want to direct and orchestrate your brand's appearance and behaviour. You can decide how to make your audience engage as effectively as possible with your brand's values and beliefs.

DIRECTING YOUR BRAND'S BEHAVIOUR AND APPEARANCE

Before we close this chapter, we would like to touch on the functions of the brand manager and the brand creative director.

The brand manager

Although we use the analogy of a brand as a person, a brand is obviously *not* a person. This is mainly because a brand is usually never under the control of just one individual. And this means that you may run the risk – if you cannot completely share your understanding of the brand with all stakeholders – of that brand becoming a "multiple personality".

That's why, to orchestrate a single, unified brand identity, it is essential that you clarify the functional accountability and responsibility for each element of that identity. You need to install clear governance and cross-functional ways of working to orchestrate both the "macro" picture (the tonality of one brand) and the "micro" level (the cluster of propositions under one brand).

You should therefore assign one brand manager (or group) to act as custodian of the brand's values, beliefs and personality and to set the framework of the brand. This manager should not only act as guardian of the brand's authenticity, but also carefully monitor the market and competitors in order to direct and stretch the brand. It is also important for this manager, or a similar brand level function, to manage the brand architecture and brand portfolio (the number of propositions offered to the market) to lead and guide the brand's entire company-wide portfolio.

We would like to point out that we believe a company CEO should be responsible and accountable on brand management.

The brand creative director

Complementing the brand manager, a brand creative director (and this can be an individual or a group of design team members) is needed to articulate the chosen brand values, beliefs and personality with the most appropriate brand behaviour and appearance. The key role for a brand creative director is the orchestration of a complete experience of the brand through the audience's interaction with, and visualization of, the brand's touchpoints.

A brand creative director should maintain a "bandwidth" of brand behaviour and appearance based on the brand architecture and portfolio. Returning to the analogy of a brand as a person, a brand creative director is an advisor on manners and behaviour, as well as a stylist who fully understands your brand's values, beliefs and personality and who can advise you on the way you appear to the public. Working from your values and beliefs, the brand creative director can specify the appropriate behaviour and "dress" for each setting (proposition portfolio) your brand appears in.

At the same time, the brand creative director should ensure that whatever your behaviour or appearance may be, it will always be recognized as belonging to one brand with one set of values and beliefs. And those behaviours and appearances must be continuously updated and adjusted (as an individual updates their behaviour and appearance) to take account of changing trends in society, culture, aesthetics and style. A brand creative director must always be fully up to date with all the changes in the society in which the brand appears.

Part 2
Know Your Audience

2
Commitment 2: Understand Short- and Long-Term Needs

If you were to ask children what they *need*, most would say toys or games such as Nintendo, or perhaps an iPod or iPad – something they currently desire. You'd be hard pressed to find a child who'd reply, "After a careful study of the fast-growing Chinese market, which will undoubtedly become even more important in the long-term, I would say that I need an education in the Chinese language."

That isn't a child's answer, because few children understand the distinction between *need* (a necessity) and *want* (something merely desired). The answer given here is more likely to come from the child's parents, whose role it is to take a long-term view; just as they must also anticipate the short-term requirements – such as adequate clothing and nutritious food – that their child may not consider, but whose effects he or she will certainly feel. They are responsible, in effect, for their child's short-term satisfaction and long-term happiness.

In the world of design, there is much the same responsibility: because if your company truly loves its audience then you will not only need to consider its short-term satisfaction, but also anticipate its long-term happiness. And you should remember that needs, especially long-term needs, are usually "latent".

Before we go any further, though, we'd like to elaborate on the different research approaches required when distinguishing people's short- and long-term needs.

DIFFERENT APPROACHES

In the short term, if they are aware of them, you can simply ask people to describe their needs. For latent needs (those they are unaware of), you can use a range of "people research techniques". These can help you discover what people are having problems with, or problems for which they've found a "workaround" solution (that they might have done "unconsciously" and which will then need to be "uncovered").

For example, when Neil managed the design team at Tesco, he was involved in the redesign of bananas! To be precise, it was the redesign of how to *sell* bananas – and yes there were even opportunities there for innovation! By observing customers, the team discovered that customers were breaking bunches of bananas apart – often without realizing that they were doing so. This resulted in damage to some bananas, which then didn't sell. Further investigation provided two insights. One was that people wanted green (to eat later) or yellow (to eat now) bananas. They also wanted a specific bunch size. The solution the team came up with was to redesign the stand. The bananas were placed in "cradles" and offered in noticeably different-sized bunches, as well as in groups of green and yellow. The results were dramatic and both increased sales and reduced waste. Tesco also developed an "eat-me/keep-me" bag of bananas with green and yellow ones combined so that the customer could eat some ripe bananas now and save some green ones for later.

By contrast, future needs are all latent since the future remains unknown. It is impossible for anyone to experience it, or to accurately predict it, since it can be influenced by completely unpredictable events. With long-term needs we cannot observe or use other research techniques, so we are forced to rely completely on the examination of "macro trends" and to "hypothesize and predict" how such trends may influence people's behaviours and attitudes. (Experts in trends observation and analysis do exist and have made the field a speciality.) We can also affect choices with "memories of the future" (something we touch on later in this chapter).

Finally it's worth noting that in both cases (short- and long-term) it's best to test any hypothesis you may have with a working prototype – something that people can experience – rather than just asking for their opinion. This might not necessarily mean a fully working prototype; you can make an experience demonstrator for one function with completely "simulated/fake" technology because it is intended only to test (by imitating a real experience) the specific benefits and functions of a concept. What's important is the *experience* it delivers. (See Chapter 12 for more on this.)

BUILDING INSIGHTS

So there's a difference between short- and long-term needs. What this means for you and your brand – if you want to bring meaningful, relevant and distinctive propositions to today's marketplace – is this: it is essential that you build up a deep insight into people's daily experience. And you must do this by looking at what's happening out on the streets around the world, at the products, events and cultural reference points that influence and inspire them. You need to understand the immediate problems people face and they way they interpret the world around them. You also need to predict – with considerable accuracy – what's going to have the most appeal in the very near long term.

Once you have gathered this information, you must then use it to provide the foundation for your design work. You must use it to identify and meet the short-term and long-term needs of your audience.

UNDERSTANDING EMOTIONS, SENSORY PERCEPTIONS AND CULTURAL VALUES

Within the context of short-term and long-term needs, it's important to generate your understanding based not only on people's behaviour and activities, but also on their emotions, sensory perceptions and cultural values – because these can ensure you know how people decode messages and propositions and therefore help you to find the best format of your proposition and how to communicate it.

Building data about people and how they experience products and services is very important for design. So is an understanding of different cultural backgrounds. As we grow older, our understanding of what we see around us increases as our knowledge and experience increase. For example, the detail of the steel rivet design – to most people – is robustness, rigidity and strength: since almost all of us have encountered similar details in steam engines and architectural constructions such as the Eiffel Tower. Our knowledge of how these objects are constructed means that we – unconsciously – perceive strength when we encounter this type of detail.

Yet such knowledge is not always universal, because it is also influenced by our cultural backgrounds: and these are not always the same.

For example, Yasushi needed to organize an event in Hong Kong and, since the same event had already been organized in several other countries, he planned to "cut and paste" the same style to the Hong Kong event. This called for the use of white as the overall colour of the event, with blue as the accent colour (since it was the official colour of Philips, where he worked) to provide a blue and white atmosphere.

However when he visited Hong Kong for preparatory discussions he met an architect friend who told him that in China the combination of blue and white denoted a funeral: hardly a suitable atmosphere for his event. So it's clear that even a very simple thing like colour can strongly denote different things to people from different cultural backgrounds.

To give one further example from Neil's past studies, consider the traditional Japanese house, which has no solid walls; it uses instead a series of screens that can be slid to one side, or even removed. It is a multifunctional space and is designed so that rooms can be used for various purposes. The climate also plays a role; because of the heat, walls can be removed to allow cooling drafts of air to flow freely. One possible indirect consequence of this is that there is no notion of "privacy" in Japan, or even an exact word for it. It is, in fact, seen as quite negative to want to be on one's own.

It's because of differences like this that designers need to continuously generate and increase their knowledge of all the world's cultural backgrounds and their various layers. It's these layers that we want to look at next.

THREE LAYERS

The Cultural Anthropology Tutorials website, created and maintained by Dr. Dennis O'Neil (of the Behavioral Sciences Department at Palomar College in San Marcos, California), has pinpointed three layers of culture that are part of our learned behaviour patterns and perceptions.

O'Neil writes about the first layer that: "Most obvious is the body of cultural traditions relating to your specific society. In this level, people share language, traditions, and beliefs that set each of these peoples apart from others."

The second layer consists of the subculture. A subculture is a mix of people's original cultural traditions in their new society; for example, many Italians who emigrated to the USA in the late nineteenth and early twentieth centuries maintained an Italian subculture, one based on customs, fashion and food unknown or unavailable in their new home. O'Neil writes that:

> In complex, diverse societies in which people have come from many different parts of the world, they often retain much of their original cultural traditions. As a result, they are likely to be part of an identifiable subculture in their new society. The shared cultural traits of subcultures set them apart from the rest of their society.

For O'Neil, the third layer can be called "cultural universals" and he describes it thus: "These are learned behaviour patterns that are shared by all of humanity collectively. No matter where people live in the world, they share these universal traits." He then goes on to offer such examples as using age and gender to classify people, or the raising children in a family setting.

It's important for design to understand all the aspects of the first and third layers: "cultural traditions" and "cultural universals". We believe most strongly that it is essential for design competence to install and maintain an on-going study of culture and trends so it can generate and build up knowledge. Design competence should scan signals and analyse emerging aesthetics, communication codes and behaviour. It should capture recent developments in the fields that manifest the early signals of the "new", such as art, fashion, interior design, architecture, cinema and new media. It should also understand how "cultural traditions" and "cultural universals" create semiotic and sensory codes of captured signals.

UNCOVERING LONG-TERM NEEDS

A brand needs to continuously innovate to ensure its long-term sustainability. People insight is the food that sustains this innovation (and technology is often the enabler). When you undertake your research into the long term, you'll quickly discover that it's a challenge to ask people to think so far ahead. But you need to do this because what you must determine are their "unmet and undiscovered (even hidden in their own minds) needs" as well as "(the social stages and development of) what is acceptable in society".

For example, we think it's fair to assume that one of the long desired unmet needs of human beings is to manage long distance communication. Many people harbour a secret desire to be Superman, able to be anywhere at any time. (It is this desire that has made him such a popular character.) During the twentieth century, the telephone and later the mobile phone were innovations designed to fulfil this need.

If we talk about the need for long-distance communication, people's unmet needs are rather obvious. But hand in hand with the solution goes a change in society and culture. And you need to consider these, too.

As we have all seen over the last twenty to thirty years of mobile phone development, society has continuously developed and adapted its behaviour and manners about the way in which they are used. For example, not so long ago, somebody seen speaking in public with the aid a hands-free phone (an even greater extension of the Superman dream) would have been regarded as mentally disturbed. Today, it's a totally normal sight.

So we wonder what the reaction would be to a company that offered to implant a microchip in our bodies that would let us make a phone call without having to lay our fingers on any device at all. You might say that most people would probably never tolerate such an implant. And you might be right. But you would also have to admit that plastic surgery is something far more accepted in society now than it was in the past. And there is one place in our bodies where nearly all of us accept implants without any hesitation: our teeth.

The point we are trying to make here is that although a solution sometimes perfectly fulfils an unmet need, it may not always be so readily accepted by society. This is why it is important not only for design competence to understand undiscovered needs but also to find an acceptable articulation for them. So although research is looking at a long-term view, it will need continuous short-term adjustment. Viewed from this perspective, uncovering long-term needs is completely different from predicting the long term. It is more like drawing a roadmap of the views we think will exist in an ideal long-term society.

DRAWING A ROADMAP OF THE LONG TERM

So how do you draw such a "long-term needs" roadmap? To begin with, you need to explore where the world and society are heading. You need to continuously collect information on such influential areas as economics, politics, the environment, technology and socio-cultural trends. Based on the information collected, you can then explore both shared and specific individual cultural values (such as prosperity, happiness, wealth, power and sustainability) and note similarities and differences between regions and generations.

You may find that this requires extensive research and is too abstract – too removed – from your business opportunities. We would answer that the roadmap doesn't always require extensive research. You could quite easily draw one, for example; for your children you will at some stage make plans for their education. To do that, you will probably use all the information available to you about economics, politics, the environment, technology and socio-cultural trends. And it may well be that you decide, from all your research and thinking, that an education in the Chinese language is important. You've created your own long-term needs roadmap.

MEMORIES OF THE FUTURE

In his earlier work Stefano Marzano (1999) noted the importance of understanding what people desire, and find relevant and meaningful, by undertaking long-term explorations. He was referring to what neuroscientists David Ingvar (1985) and William Calvin (1995) have called "memories of the future". Stefano said:

> David Ingvar and William Calvin suggest that failure to undertake such future-gazing is one sure way to be taken by surprise. Thinking about potential future developments opens your mind, so that you're ready to see the signs relevant to those developments if and when they occur.
>
> ...
>
> Ingvar, for instance, found that part of the brain is constantly making up action plans and programmes for the future, organised along time paths and with alternatives for various situations. He found that these plans are stored in the brain, along with memories of real experiences – which is why he calls them "memories of the future". He suggests that this not only helps us make decisions when we have to, but, more importantly, it helps us filter information. We only take notice of incoming information that fits in with one of our alternative plans. Conversely, if we have no alternative plans, we fail to notice things because they don't seem to be relevant to anything.
>
> Stefano Marzano, 1999

Stefano continued by saying:

> The same principle applies at both company and consumer level. At company level, if we have not formulated a number of options in advance, our eyes will not be focused: we will be looking in all directions

and see nothing. And we'll find it difficult to discuss
alternatives with each other because we have no common points of reference. The future scenarios we
develop at Philips Design are intended to provide such
points of reference.

At consumer level, by sharing our scenarios with the
public in the form of visualisations of potential products, we get two sorts of benefit. First, we get feedback on the suitability of our scenarios. And second,
we plant "memories of the future" in people's minds,
suggesting possibilities to them that may ultimately
turn into new aspirations and wants.

Stefano pointed out that he believes long-term predictions
rarely turn into reality, that the future is not just an extension of the past and that it never happens in a consistent
and sequential manner. However he believes that the
future is made by the interplay of all activities and direction people take on a day-to-day basis, which obviously
are hugely influenced by positive and negative natural
events; because he strongly believes the future is largely
made by people!

> The future does not just happen. It is created by those
> who take on the responsibility for it today. If we are
> to look forward to a period in the future in which we
> have a stable environment and can pursue sustainable
> growth, then we must try to restore the balance in
> both our natural environment and our social and cul-
> tural environment... But first we need to get a clearer
> picture of the world we want to reach, of routes we
> could follow to get there – and of where we are today.
> Stefano Marzano, 1992

If we accept his theory, then the articulation of a long term
will offer a clear and shared focus for a company's intention,

outlook and roadmap (how to reach to the intended goal) that will fill the gap between innovation and operational excellence. It will be a roadmap that provides a company with the information it needs to anticipate, and design for, the long term.

VITAL INGREDIENTS

Before we close this chapter, we would like to make one last point and describe – briefly – two tools that will help you effectively utilize the insights you've gained into people.

We can't recommend strongly enough that you involve a multidisciplinary team in the actions you take to generate your knowledge of long-term needs. Obviously, you will need to ask your skilled researchers to conduct this activity, but it is extremely important – and very valuable to them – for all disciplines to be involved in the process. It is also a good idea to install an IT tool that enables your team to post any valuable information they discover – at any time – so it can be shared instantly with others in your organization. (For more about this, see Chapter 15.)

As for the tools, they are the *persona* and the *end-user journey*.

Persona

The *persona* is a widely known and very useful tool in the design process. Simply put, it is a fictional person to which has been added the data you need to design a product that people will want to buy: for example, values, motivations, needs, desires, hopes and dreams related to the relevant design context. You can construct a persona for business-to-consumer and business-to-business markets. Once constructed, it will provide you with the data you need to gain insights into your target audience throughout the design process.

With the aid of co-creation data, you can base your personas on real people and then watch them "grow" as you
increase the information about them day by day (just as
real human beings increase their knowledge and experience during their daily lives). By pinpointing similarities
and differences in their cultures, values and motivations, a
persona will give you a more "granular" understanding of
people; an understanding not possible with conventional
segmentation models.

End-user journey

The *end-user journey* tool enables you to visualize – and
map on a flow diagram – people's experience with products
and services. It can help you discover short-term problems in
such activities as accessing a service or vacuuming a house.
Or, when you extend it to the long term, you can focus on
specific life-changing periods; for example, when trying to
understand how an individual's short-term and long-term
needs are transformed after they decide to begin a family.

In both cases, the journeys are based on the five "engagement steps" of imagination, impression, discovery, use and
memory, under the four "experience contexts" of people, activity, location and time. (For more about this, see Chapter 4.)

The end-user journey tool enables you to capture and
synthesize people's experiences. With the information you
gather, you can then identify immediate improvement
points for usability, or analyse and identify people's
un-met needs. And you can always enrich the resulting
map by applying your people research data.

3
Commitment 3: Co-Create with People

Many neuroscientists have pointed out that when people need to describe their emotions in words they often make mistakes. To put it another way, when you ask people what they think, they tend to say something different from what they actually feel, something that doesn't reflect their "gut" emotion.

Neil once came across a case study in which the early prototype of a keyboard was tested with a potential user. The keyboard had a "bounce", meaning that it jumped up and down as the user pressed the keys. The user was filmed as he typed and, while he said that he really liked the keyboard, the video showed a very different story – clear discomfort on his face.

Similarly, in an article Yasushi once read by a very experienced dealer in exotic cars in Japan, the author claimed that he had been in the business for several decades and had realized that most buyers of Porsches said they bought them because they were practical cars to drive. (The article was written before Porsche introduced the Cayenne and the Panamera.) The buyers said they thought the cars were practical because they had rear seats that could hold two people (even though they would have had to have been under seven or even five years of age to fit comfortably in them); had plenty of room for luggage (although when Yasushi showed the front luggage space of the 911 to his wife at a show room – in an effort to persuade her that they should buy one – she laughed out loud); or some other practical reason. It seemed that few if any buyers simply said they bought them because of the beautiful design, the wonderful performance or the strong brand image that reflected positively on them. It was an example of people saying something totally different to their gut emotion.

This might be explained by what we believe cognitive scientists call "system 1" and "system 2". This comes from dual process theory, which shows how a phenomenon can occur in two different ways, or as a result of two different processes. Often the two processes consist of an implicit (automatic), unconscious process and an explicit (controlled), conscious process. Verbalized explicit processes or attitudes and actions may change with persuasion or education; though implicit process or attitudes usually take a long time to change with the forming of new habits. Dual process theories can be found in social, personality, cognitive and clinical psychology.

In his recent book *Thinking Fast and Slow* Daniel Kahneman (2012) provided further interpretation by differentiating the two styles of processing more, calling them intuition and reasoning. Intuition (or system 1), similar to associative reasoning, was determined to be fast and automatic, usually with strong emotional bonds included in the reasoning process. Kahneman said that this kind of reasoning was based on formed habits and very difficult to change or manipulate. Reasoning (or system 2) was slower and much more volatile, being subject to conscious judgements and attitudes.

As we understand them, system 1 relates to the fast and intuitive gut responses and heuristics more strongly related to the primitive brain, while system 2 is slow, effortful, conscious, rule-based and more strongly related to the slower, cognitive rationalization of the cortex that developed around the primitive brain as humans evolved. The conflict between the two might explain why people make "emotional" gut decisions and then "post-rationalize" them: sometimes confirming an emotional decision by trying to come up with rational reasons, and sometimes fighting against it, perhaps because it's not what they want, or perhaps because it's not what they think someone else wants.

FINDING OUT WHAT PEOPLE REALLY THINK

So, if people often say something that doesn't match their gut emotion, how can we really find out what they think? One way to overcome this problem is by applying neuroscience methodology to market research – by watching people's brain activity instead of their words. There are a number of interesting books available (such as *Predictably Irrational* by Dan Ariely (2008) and *Buyology* by Martin Lindstrom (2009)), which explain people's (irrational) behaviour, decision making and reactions from a neuroscientific point of view.

Although we are fascinated with this type of research, we were a little suspicious when we heard about a test of brain activity that was to be conducted with the aid of an MR scanner. If you have ever been in an MR scanner you will know how abnormal a situation it is: surrounded by noise and darkness while lying inside a narrow hole. This made us wonder how accurate an answer would be obtained from people placed in this type of environment and asked, for example, about their preference regarding Coke versus Pepsi.

However in 2011 came news that Hitachi had introduced a headset with an optical sensor to measure pre-frontal bloodstreams. And this led us to believe that the application of neuroscience in one-to-one people research would become standard in the very near future. As Malcolm Gladwell (2010) noted in his book *Blink*, most if not all people post-rationalize their feelings when asked to describe them. Neuroscientific data would then very likely help a brand to look into the feelings behind people's words by being collected from their brain activity.

But does this mean that measuring the prefrontal bloodstream is the only way to come closer to people's gut emotions? No. We believe there is one other way to do it: by the creation of an emotional engagement. We believe that if you can establish an emotional engagement with your audiences, you can get a little closer to the real feelings (emotion) behind their words. And to do that you should make use of the co-creation method. For us, one of the most important factors of co-creation work is the building of a relationship in which people can feel safe and relaxed enough to talk in a manner as close as possible to their real feelings.

DEFINING CO-CREATION

Most teenagers usually have one or a few very close friends they spend almost every moment with and whom they understand implicitly. Even when we were teenagers (now a long time ago), and without any smart phones or even the internet (with just a telephone attached to a fixed line, which meant hiding from our parents so we could talk freely), we felt extremely close to our friends almost all the time. And they probably understood our emotions and reactions far better than our parents. Although there was still the hurdle of having to translate those emotions into words, (since none of us owned the head gear that would come later from Hitachi) when we were together we managed to truly engage emotionally with each other. Can you imagine therefore what it would be like if your brand was able to have the same relationship with your audiences as you had with your friends in your teenage years?

This leads us to our definition of "co-creation" (which, although it is a well-known term these days, is used by many people in different ways). Obviously it means "creating together". But for us creating together and involving people in a certain milestone or phase of your business or product creation process are two different activities. To create together, it is important to create an emotional engagement with your audiences on a permanent basis. The key to effective co-creation is the installation of a "permanent" infrastructure that enables you to maintain a continuous connection with your audiences. This is, as we hope you can imagine, far more valuable to you than the purchase of some anonymous "people-focused data", because it represents the power of true emotional engagement. For we believe the actual asset of a brand are not the data themselves but full access to, and engagement with, your users and customers. (We should also note that this is valid not only in the business-to-consumer field but also in business-to-business areas. In fact it is actually more relevant in business-to-business areas since you can use it to leverage, and then empower, your customer relationship network and activities.)

You can co-create with people both physically (for example, by observing them within physical contexts; by running a session with business-to-business stakeholders to co-create an end-user or customer journey); or digitally, with the aid of social media (for example, by asking people to post images and video clips or stories of their cooking environment, culture and habits to a dedicated blog site).

THE KEYS TO CO-CREATION

If we accept that co-creation is the creation of an emotional engagement with your audiences on a permanent basis, then there are two key issues to consider when starting it.

The first is achieving emotional engagement. The second is keeping it on a permanent basis.

So how do you create an emotional engagement similar to the afore-mentioned teenage friendships between your brand and your audiences? Let's begin by looking into the quality and value of friendships. In its entry on "friendship", Wikipedia lists the following key attributes:

- The tendency to desire what is best for the other

- Sympathy and empathy

- Honesty, perhaps in situations where it may be difficult for others to speak the truth, especially in terms of pointing out the perceived faults of one's counterpart

- Mutual understanding and compassion; ability to go to each other for emotional support

- Enjoyment of each other's company

- Trust in one another

- Positive reciprocity – a relationship is based on equal give-and-take between the two parties

- The ability to be oneself, express one's feelings and make mistakes without fear of judgement.

You can, we hope, immediately see some important attributes that need to be fulfilled to meet the requirements for a true friendship: sympathy and empathy, honesty, mutual understanding and compassion on a topic and trust. Therefore if you can manage to fulfil these values with your audiences then you can manage to build an emotional engagement with them, too.

One way to co-create is to build an active community of people you can interact with on specific topics – an open and transparent community where people can share their enthusiasm about the topics they are engaged with. This will make it possible for you to create an on-going engagement with the right people. We are repeating ourselves here, but it is only to emphasize that the key to creating a genuine community and achieving a true collaboration means that you must be open and transparent about your goals and in dealing with that community.

Now, although we are not specialists in research methodologies, we believe it is fairly simple to start up co-creation activities through social media. For us, the most difficult thing is not how to do this but how to maintain it – in other words, how to continue your community permanently! If you want to start co-creating, then you *must* commit yourself to keeping this community alive. If you are unable to do this, we would suggest not even launching such an activity, since your inability to maintain it would seriously damage your brand perception.

You can start your community by recruiting people through social media sites. Stimulate them first through a discussion of the topics you want to consider (and remember – experience is highly personal, memorable and involving). It is also important to create a platform that enables everyone in the community to debate with each other. And, in addition to stimuli online, you can also entice people by organizing some physical material to challenge them. One way to do this is with an event (or events). This will enable you to work together by giving the participants the opportunity to express their thinking and feeling on subjects in a playful manner.

The combination of digital and physical engagement will also increase the intimacy of your community. And it is obviously important to ensure that each event and work package is well-designed, as well as fun and challenging. You can then follow up an event by sending a series of work packages to each participant to keep the momentum of their motivation going.

In Philips, who we once worked for, we saw some successful pilots in the construction of such a social community and were surprised to learn that many people not only came considerable distances to attend but also gave up their free time to do so. (We should stress that they were not paid to participate.) People came because they were excited by the proposal and looking for an occasion to share and express their thinking on a subject.

STOP MAKING A CONVENTIONAL REPORT

All the data you gather should translate into such "design tools" as persona and end-user or customer journeys. (This is explained in more detail in Chapter 2.) You should then explore your findings in experience scenarios (as described in Chapter 11). Do not ask your team to make and deliver any conventional analytical reports because such reports cannot be effectively applied to the design process. (In fact, we would go so far as to say that all of the conventional reports we have seen are generally useless to the design process and a waste of all the rich insights you generate.)

Moreover, as we noted in Chapter 2, an additionally effective way to fully utilize research data is through the creation of a multidisciplinary team during the research activities. Obviously, your expert virtuoso should lead and conduct the research activity based on valid and proven methodologies, but it should always be conducted under the leadership of the maestro and should also involve all other disciplines throughout the research process – so that every stakeholder can start to build up their knowledge and anticipate how to utilize the data during the next steps of your design activity. It is up to the respective maestro – who leads the total design activities for the domain and/or category – to ensure that all the virtuosos are clearly aware of the requirements and demands of other disciplines (on virtuoso and maestro see Chapter 13).

SERVE AND LEARN WITH YOUR COMMUNITY

The co-creation approach is a step forward from observational-based research. And it can also – or, we should say, should be – organized as a part of your full touchpoint strategy. By doing this, your community can operate on a permanent basis.

For example, Forrester Research, Inc. – an independent global research and advisory firm – created a diagram of digital touch-points that visualized the experiences (various activities like discover, search, use, get help, etc.) of multiple customers and the potential digital media that could be utilized to enable them. Note that any co-creation activities should also be part of your brand's total social media strategy and plan. This will ensure that you can continuously – and interactively – serve and learn from your community during every moment and touchpoint of the customer's journey.

Design Council "Design Leadership Programme" Case Study – Whittington Hospital

The Design Council runs the Design Leadership Programme, which offers a bespoke package of support and coaching to use design to innovate and grow. The programme has led more than 2000 organizations in the private and public sectors to growth. Neil has been involved in this from the early days as a design strategist and more recently as an associate of the Design Council contracted to deliver coaching on the programmes.

- It has turned around businesses in manufacturing, services, retail, and research and development.

- It has transformed the way many local authorities deliver services in health, housing, communities and environment.

• It has supported science and technology innovations to accelerate their ideas to market.

Before the Design Leadership Programme, 55% of
organizations thought design was integral or important to their business.
  After the programme, 98% said design was integral
or important to their business.
  The programme has delivered an average of £20
increased turnover for every £1 invested in design by
small and medium sized businesses (the target audience of the business programme). (See http://www.
designcouncil.org.uk/our-work/leadership/ for more
information.)

The Whittington Hospital in north London was one
of the participants in the programme. The Whittington
serves a diverse community of around 450,000 people. One of its key aims is to ensure outpatient care
standards are maintained and that care is customer
focused and efficient. To explore how to make its services more user-centred, Whittington decided to focus
first on its outpatient pharmacy.
  Patients, often unwell and anxious, had to queue in
a poorly lit room, and did not know how long they
would have to wait for their prescriptions. Chief phar-
macist, Dr Helen Taylor, was keen to understand how
design might support service efficiency to better meet
the needs of the 200 to 300 patients served daily. Her
team had previously carried out user surveys but this
failed to produce insights due to lack of participation.
  She approached the Design Council's Design
Leadership Programme, which paired her with design
associates Sean Miller and Anna White.

They identified three areas where design could enhance the service:

- Improve the experience for patients
- Use every intervention as a health promotion opportunity
- Develop a retail offer to offset capital expenditure.

Miller kicked off with a workshop to introduce core design concepts to key stakeholder groups including patients, pharmacy staff, doctors and representatives from senior management. Dr Taylor said:

> The workshops taught us new ways to get patient feedback and made us realize that we needed to find out not only what, but also why and how. It initially seemed a much messier process but in fact was much richer and far more effective.

Miller then worked with a larger group to help them create a shared definition of the problem. They mapped customer experiences and spent time with customers to develop "personas". This enabled them to develop tangible improvement opportunities, which formed the basis of a brief.

Miller used the brief to help Whittington select design agency TILT and service design agency Commonground to deliver the project in partnership. The two agencies ran a series of workshops looking at issues such as flexible zoning and helped partici-pants turn ideas into full-scale cardboard prototypes, mocking up seating areas, changing the service desk's position and making other changes to the space.

Prototypes were tested live in the pharmacy with patients. Patient feedback was then used to modify the designs – co-creating the solutions together.

Through this work, the group generated a set of recommendations, including moving the service desk to improve flow, improved prescription tracking information for patients and new areas for confidential consultations. These have been approved by the hospital's project board.

Dr Taylor explained:

> As we get funding for different bits, we just implement them. Management feels strongly that we should just push things through because it has such a good effect on patients.

Senior management has endorsed the approach for other outpatient areas and has decided to apply it to the ambulatory care service on a larger scale. The pharmacy will continue to prototype new changes with patients.

Dr Taylor continued:

> The key thing for me was the way we were able to engage patients during the live process. Once we started doing the prototyping, we got so much feedback. It was completely different from the questionnaire process.

What also stood out for us in this case study was the "buy in" gained from the staff. When it comes to services, co-creating with staff and customers gains their commitment to what you are all trying to achieve, as a result it is more likely you get better engagement and customer service – which is essential as service delivery staff are a key brand touchpoint, especially in businesses more weighted towards service.

One of the challenges in designing and delivering great service is that you are much more dependent, compared with the world of manufactured products, on the staff that deliver it. Unless the team who are delivering the service really believe that every detail matters, they're not going to be creating the best experience for customers. That's where the methods of co-creation are especially powerful, to ensure that the values of the brand are embodied in the service design, so that the service team find it easy, hopefully enjoyable to deliver the service experience.

Mat Hunter,
Chief Design Office, Design Council

WHY CO-CREATION?

For us, the key advantage of co-creation is that you can change from being a "receiver and observer" of insights – someone who purchases anonymous data or only observes an audience without interacting with it – to a "leader and stimulator" – someone who generates insights that not only apply to a design and business approach but also truly inspire all cross function teams. And with that in mind, we would like to close this chapter by describing three ways to enrich your co-creation research:

- Build a community
- Lead and stimulate your community
- Make your community interactive.

Build a community

Instead of just receiving data or talking to people on the street for one-only observational research, create an active community of people you can interact with on specific topics. This will make it possible for you to create an on-going engagement with the right people. But note that to create a genuine community and achieve a true collaboration, *you* will need to be open and transparent about your goals and purpose with the community. At a later stage, you can extend the role of this community to other activities through the business creation process, even right up to a marketing launch. (For example, if you want to highlight real people in your marketing communications, this community could be one of your key resources.)

Lead and stimulate your community

Instead of observing people and collecting data, you should stimulate the participants so that they really share their motivations, values, beliefs and true experiences with you. Challenge their imagination and curiosity so that they think and interact together on selected subjects.

Make your community interactive

Instead of asking questions, organize a session that is truly interactive. (And don't forget to stimulate people by organizing an event that is open and playful.) This will help the community participate in the creation of ideas that are truly relevant and meaningful for them.

4

Commitment 4: Understand *How* People Experience

In order to take a people-focused approach, it is essential for you to understand *how* people experience the events in their lives. Let's start with the *Concise Oxford English Dictionary* definition of "experience":

- Actual observation of or practical acquaintance with facts or events

- Knowledge or skill resulting from this

- An event regarded as affecting one

- The fact or process of being so affected.

Experiences can range from the "small scale" (feeding milk to a baby) to "large scale" (raising a child) and we always experience them in terms of time. We are aware of causes and effects. We realize that one event will lead to another, and that events will merge into an overall experience. We have certain expectations of what should and shouldn't happen at some events, such as a birthday for example. We're surprised if an event we're familiar with leads to an unexpected result and we are disappointed if an experience doesn't match up to our expectation. This is how we have learned about, and come to understand, the world. And that is why, when we recall or describe our experiences, we recall them as stories, sequences of contexts, interactions and events that flow together in a meaningful fashion and trigger our emotions.

> What does an experience involve? First of all, it takes place over time; it's revealed gradually. We can divide it up into at least four sequential phases: Impression, Discovery, Use and Memory.
>
> Stefano Marzano, 1999

We have further built on his thinking and descriptions of four stages of the experience by adding the imagination phase. To better understand, explain and make use of this flow, let us explain five separate stages of experience: imagination, impression, discovery, use and memory (Note: the experience design thinking and description of stages were developed by Philips Design with many people involved between 1990 to 2012.)

Imagination.   This refers to the way people imagine what they will experience, based either on information they may have received, or their own memories. At any time during this stage, expectation (positive or negative) can hugely influence an individual's perception of what happens next. For example, a book you have been told is wonderful may disappoint because it fails to live up to your high expectations.

Impression.   An individual's first impression at the beginning of an experience can govern whether they are willing to continue to engage with it. Impressions are affected by expectations, which are governed by memory and cultural references. We've probably all heard the phrase, "You can't judge a book by its cover"; however, that said, the cover might be the first impression you have of a book and it might persuade you to begin to read.

Discovery.   This is the point at which a person begins to actively engage with the experience and discover more. They are learning how to exist within the experience.

Returning to the example of a book, it's the moment when you leaf through a few pages, read the text on the back cover or study the contents to decide whether you want to invest in buying and reading it.

Use. This describes the moment an individual takes an active role in the experience, when they become fully engaged and immersed "in the moment". For example, when you are reading a book you enjoy, the rest of the world falls away as it envelops you within its world.

Memory. Based on their previous experiences, their memories and their understanding of the cultural context they are in, people will have certain expectations that will also influence the overall experience. What we remember will be influenced by similar experiences we have had. For example, we will judge a party by other parties we have been to, concerts by other concerts we have attended and books by other books we have read.

With the help of these five stages, we would now like to walk you through an actual experience, and in the process analyse further how it is "constructed". Since it is a hobby of Yasushi's, we want to use the example of wine tasting, written from his point of view.

DISCOVERING WINERIES – FROM IMAGINATION TO MEMORY

Visiting a winery and sampling its wines, in the very place where they are made, is a wonderful experience, even for those who are not necessarily wine lovers. This is the way Yasushi usually goes about it. He wrote:

Making plans

Although it is fun to visit a winery on the spur of the moment, I usually plan all of my visits in advance and make appointments to do so. This is a sensible step for

wineries in Bordeaux and Bourgogne in France, especially
if you want to visit a specific location. The wineries in
Alsace, Germany and Austria are more "open door", so
you have more chance of being able to drop in without an
appointment. I mention all this because, for me, the wine
tasting experience starts when I begin making plans for a
visit. And in addition to making appointments, I usually
prepare information about the wines I expect to taste from
books and magazines to which I subscribe. So while I am
doing all this research my trip has actually started – in my
imagination.

It's also worth noting that if you have already visited a
location, then what you imagine will be more tangible
(your memory will make use of all your senses – not just
sight but also smell and sound etc.). If you have not yet
been there, then reviewing all available photos and descriptions – and these days you can even walk around a location
without going there by using Google Street View – will
enable you to travel to the place in your imagination. This
is always my first step in a wine tasting experience.

Raising expectations

In any winery, I always love to walk through the vineyards. It is what I call "a full sense experience". By being
in the actual place where the wine makers grow their
grapes, by feeling the sun and the wind on my skin, by
breathing the air and touching the soil, I can realize my
expectations to the fullest. Even just seeing them from a
distance is a pleasure. Some are large, well-maintained
chateaus, while others are modest farm houses. Either
way, seeing them gives me some expectation about the
types of wines made there.

And although it has nothing to do with the taste of the
actual wine, interacting with the staff or the owner makes
another impression. (Some wineries employ a part-time guide

to show you around, while in others the owner acts as your guide.) So does walking through the winery and seeing the type of equipment being used: it offers another clue about the winery's attitude to the type of wine it wants to make. Then, finally, you are invited to the tasting room – sometimes a nicely designed, purpose-built space; sometimes just a part of the cellar. (One winery had set up table and chairs outside so that, while the wines were being tasted there was a full view of its vineyards.) Whatever the location, such details add colour and texture to any wine tasting.

Observing a wine

In any wine tasting, there are two steps you must take before you enjoy the actual taste. The first is to observe the appearance of the wine by looking at it. This enables you to check its clarity, limpidity, viscosity and brilliance, which shows you the "style" of the wine. The next step is to smell the aroma. In order to do that, you must first swirl the wine around in the glass. This is a technique for deliberately aerating the wine as forcefully as possible. After you swirl the wine, you put your nose into the glass and inhale deeply. This is always an important first impression: it enables you to experience the complexity of the aromas and how well they all blend together. Only when you have done all of this do you take your fist sip.

The first sip

Although I always attended a number of wine tastings, one thing I am bad at is spitting out the wine. Since I am not a professional who needs to taste 100 or so wines a day, I always drink all the samples I am given. As you no doubt know, nose and mouth are connected (if you block your nose, you really cannot enjoy the full flavour of any foods or drinks) but your tongue enables you to differentiate taste between sweetness, sourness, fruitiness and so on. So after smelling the wine, you take the next step in the experience by sipping it. And when you take that first sip, your mouth goes through three stages: first attack (when the wine enters your mouth), then expansion (when the wine fills your mouth) and then the aftermath (when you either swallow or spit out the wine).

Five senses' memory

Of the many memorable wine-tasting visits I have made with my wife and friends, one in particular stands out for me. It was a visit to Domain Michel Lafarge in Volnay, in France's Bourgogne district. I didn't know how to contact the winery in advance so, one rainy day in October, I knocked on the owner's door, without an appointment. He spoke very little English (and no one in the party could speak any French), but when I showed him a Japanese wine magazine with an illustrated article about his winery and explained that we had come from Japan to visit him he let us in, showed us around and allowed us to sample his wines. Even though the owner spoke French and I spoke English, we somehow managed to communicate. It was a most memorable visit, so much so that whenever there is a slight rain I can still smell the air in Volnay, and remember the typical mouldy odour of the wine cellar. When I drink one of his wines, all these memories – and sights and sounds and smells – come flooding back immediately.

RESEARCHING EXPERIENCE

The wine tasting is Yasushi's own personal experience. What you, as designers, need to do is to understand the experiences of others in as much detail, to gather as much useful information as possible. The final sections of this chapter are intended to offer advice about how to do just that: to conduct effective, illuminating research.

SET THE CONTEXTS OF EXPERIENCE WHEN YOU CONDUCT RESEARCH

When you generate insights into people's experience during the five engagement steps described at the beginning of the chapter, it is important to specify the experience you are trying to uncover by using the following aspects of the context setting:

People

- Who is your target audience? Does it include multiple stakeholders or individual actions? It is important to understand each person's role, attitudes, values and beliefs, rituals, habits and so on in context.

Activity

- What is your target doing? It's important to understand the goal and motivation of activities in context. It's also important to understand cultural habits and beliefs, as well as current and emerging trends related to specific activities.

Location

- Where is this activity taking place? It's important to understand places/spaces and their surroundings in context. It's also important to understand the current and emerging trends related to the specific locations.

Time

- What is the time frame? Is it short (feeding milk to baby) or long (raising a child)?

Only by clearly setting the context of the experience can you clearly frame the type of insights you want to generate.

AN EXPERIENCE IS HIGHLY PERSONAL

It is important to realize that an experience is a personal perception and, as such, can never be created or engineered by others. As we have already said, experience is very closely connected to perception, memory, cultural reference and expectation.

What this means is that, in addition to understanding the five stages of engagement involved in an experience, you must also understand an individual's background, and the different cultural models that influence their perception and meaning, before you can begin to design an experience for them. You must always focus on people.

AN EXPERIENCE BUILDS UP OVER TIME

When you find a good restaurant, one that gave you an enjoyable time and a good memory, you will probably go back to it again. And every time you go back, your expectations will grow and change. For example, you may expect the staff to remember your name or to recommend specific dishes and wines because they're familiar with your tastes. This doesn't mean that you expect more service but rather that you expect an increased personalization of your experience. Repeated aspects of the quality that you appreciated during your first experience will confirm your appreciation of this restaurant, but more "personalized" engagements will add another level of satisfaction with it.

(If you are in the service industry and have face-to-face contact with your customers, this is something you either do naturally or structurally by collecting data about your customers. Today, due to the availability of connected touchpoints – for example, social media – it's now possible to collect data about your end-users and customers that enable you to both satisfy and delight by not only fulfilling their expectations, but also by exceeding their expectations.) The challenge for design is to make these data useful for your internal company staff and to enable them to act on the data to deliver a better and more personalized experience: one that not only fulfils expectations but also continuously delights your end-users and customers. (A key measure in much of the service industry is ARPU – Average Revenue per User. It's indicative of the desire to build up a long-term, on-going relationship that increases in value over time.)

AN EXPERIENCE IS MEMORABLE AND INVOLVING

As we have already stated, we believe an experience is a personal perception and, as such, can never be created or engineered by others. This is because an experience is built up by an individual's continuous personal choices in the particular context of that experience.

A former colleague of ours, Thomas Marzano, who is an expert in social media, said that if you want to get more traffic to your blog site then you need to ask people to participate. For example, instead of telling them about "The top ten of 80s music" it would be better to say, "Let's vote for the top ten of 80s music". It's a good example of how to design an experience: by *involving* people.

Over the last few years, some brands have tried to build an offer of several choices into their product and services. For example, more than five years ago Dell and Nike began to offer a kind of mass customization. Dell allows you to select particular features or configurations from a number of options at the moment of purchase; Nike lets you specify the colours and symbols on your running shoes. The car industry has offered this type of "mass customization" for even longer. However (except for some premium car makers who offer customers the full freedom to chose *any* colours) this is only customization. It's not really personalization (offering complete flexibility in tailoring a product to meet an individual's personal desires), because the options are limited to those prescribed by the maker or supplier and, in the case of Dell and Nike, must be specified before the sale and cannot be altered later.

More sophisticated possibilities can be seen in the current trend of smart phones and mobile phone apps, which 1) enable consumers to make the customization themselves, and 2) then let them adapt them to their own purposes *after* the moment of sale. (This also, incidentally, offers the brand an opportunity to continue a dialogue with customers after the phone has been purchased.)

AN EXPERIENCE IS DEFINED BY MEMORY

Memory is used continuously during an experience to interpret perceptions, create expectations and help understand what is going on. An individual's memory contains their previous personal experiences and their interpretation of a shared cultural reference. That memory has been built up over the course of an entire lifetime and represents a filter for understanding things the individual encounters in the world. So when an individual encounters a place, object or situation then – in addition to what their senses tell them – they will draw on their memories to help them evaluate the experience. Research suggests that only 20% of an experience can be credited to the senses. The remaining 80% is a result of an individual's own cognitive process of interpretation.

Memory is also affected and developed during the experience. As we have already pointed out, experiences are often described as the things that have happened to you that influence the way you think and behave. That's why an individual's memory will change based on their first impression of (for example) a product, how they learned about what it does and how they use it over time.

AN EXPERIENCE RELIES ON PERSONAL AND CULTURAL REFERENCES

In Chapter 2, we discussed the importance of understanding cultural references. Everyone has their own references, and they influence our expectations, mindset, perceptions, meaning and emotions. Such references come from personal experiences, but they are also influenced by others who share a similar background or who have participated in the same events. This is why it's important for design to fully understand cultural and generational symbols, semiotics, habits and rituals.

For example, if you are invited to another person's house in Japan and are offered coffee or tea and perhaps something to eat, you usually say first, "Okamai naku", ("You do not need to take care of me"). However this is something you say as a part of ritual; the host will still serve the refreshments offered. Yet were we to respond with the same words in the Netherlands, we would probably be offered nothing; the host would take our words at face value. It's a small but vivid demonstration of the differences between cultures and therefore between habits, rituals and understandings.

AN EXPERIENCE IS PERCEIVED THROUGH THE SENSES

When we experience something, we usually use all our senses: sight, sound, touch, smell and taste. The context for an experience is composed of multiple sensory impressions.

One of the best books on the engagement of multiple senses is *Brand Sense* by Martin Lindstrom (2010). As he points out, there are few brands that have managed to fully utilize multiple senses to create a brand experience with people. For us, one of the best examples he offers is the sound Daimler Chrysler established in 1990s for its car doors: "A team of ten engineers was mandated to analyse and then implement the perfect sound of a car door, whether it was opening or closing."

It goes without saying that a door is the one thing you always need to use when you use your car. And every time you open and close it the sound the door makes will continuously confirm the quality of the car: it will enter your ears and make its way into your memory, and this memory will be associated with the brand of your car.

Many scientists believe that smell is the only one of our senses directly hardwired to our brains. We also assume they are, initially, triggering our system 1 (as described at the beginning of Chapter 3). This may explain why smells themselves can be such a very powerful trigger. (Just one whiff of an old classroom can instantly transport you back to your school days, while many people can distinctly remember the smell of their new car or the perfume of an old flame.) It would explain why, today, specialist companies are offering scent creation as a service and some retailers are using smells to trigger brand recognition. During the writing of this book, for example, we noticed that our local H&M store always smelled of cinnamon, with the result that that we now almost always associate cinnamon with H&M. (It's worth noting that there are companies at work today whose business it is to provide your brand with a specific smell.) The US Abercrombie and Fitch stores take this principle one step further. They use a signature scent called FIERCE that is sprayed through automatic sprayers in their flagship store on a regular basis. So if you buy any item of clothing it smells very strongly of the scent and reminds you of the brand long after you've left the store.

The senses are our interface with the physical world. The signals we receive through sight, sound, touch, smell and taste are then interpreted by our brains into meaning and experience. And our perceptions of meaning and experience are, as we have already described, filtered and influenced by our memories and cultural references. It is therefore the task of design to increase its knowledge of people's perceptions of the signals they receive through each sense. And it is also important that design learns to master the orchestration of all of these signals, either separately or together.

Case Study – Philips–Alessi

Let us share one of the best cases of how to design an experience. Stefano Marzano (1999) described how to design an experience.

So how do we design an experience? It really all comes down to how you look at your product. If you look at it as a machine – a good – you focus on its features, and you design it with those in mind. If you look at it as the carrier of a service, you focus on the quality of the resulting service or benefits and how to enhance them. But if you view the product as a part of an experience, you focus on creating a total experience, and making it as engaging as possible.

He continued by saying:

Take a coffee maker, for instance. Suppose you don't consider it in terms of a product with features, but in terms of the delicious cup of coffee it provides you with. The centre of gravity of the product has shifted from being a good to being a service. The next step is to see this service taking place within a larger context – enjoying a special moment. By focusing on the user's total experience in this way, we find new aspects of the product that we can improve for them.

In this speech, he shared one of the projects where he applied this thinking.

We applied this concept when we launched the Philips–Alessi kitchen appliances. For an experience to work its magic, you must get consumers to the starting point: the Impression Phase. One way to achieve this is to get media and opinion leaders to impress them for us. So we designed a "Philips–Alessi Experience" especially for them. ...

Their impression phase began when we aroused their curiosity through mysterious photos of the products, and by announcing that this launch would "rehumanize" the kitchen. The launch also took place in a museum that was not yet open, the Groningen Museum, designed by Alessandro Mendini.

The Philips–Alessi preview

The Discovery phase started when the journalists and opinion leaders entered this unique museum. Inside, they were surrounded by a multi-screen environment that first exposed them to an evocation of a noisy, stress-filled way of life, and then changed to restful images and the sound of running water, the aroma of coffee and the smell of toasted bread. After a brief introduction, the guests were led by actors, dressed to symbolize the products, to where they could use the products and sip coffee, make toast, squeeze fresh juice, all amid a setting of fragrant coffee beans and images of orange groves.

Philips–Alessi launch at the Groningen Museum

Finally, as the Memory phase, guests were presented with a gift book, La Cucina Elettrica (The Electric Kitchen).

The Memory phase for the Philips–Alessi experience

This whole event – essentially a theatrical performance – resulted in a great deal of free publicity. This, combined with specially designed point-of-purchase displays, created a 'first impression' for the general public, encouraging them to embark on their Discovery phase. The products sold well, becoming design icons and appearing as background décor in third-party ads, commercials and TV shows.

...

The Use and Memory phases finally led to the products becoming collectors' items and helped reposition the Philips brand in the minds of consumers.

Note: about the Philips–Alessi project

The Philips–Alessi line of appliances was launched in 1994. This collaboration enabled Philips to establish its image as a design innovator, while Alessi learned how to expand into the field of electrical equipment. Both benefited from the extension, and consumers benefited by getting the more colourful, human kitchens they had wanted. The Philips–Alessi line basically set the trend for the rest of the decade. Stefano ideated the collaboration as strategy to reposition the Philips brand in small appliances: what he named later on the "elevator strategy". Associating with a brand with a higher positioning is an accelerator of brand positioning.

UNDERSTAND AND DECODE

If you truly want to deliver the ideal, full experience to your audience – especially if you want to exceed their expectations and show your true love – you must do two things. You must understand the "context" (the person, activity, place and time). And you must decode the mechanisms of experience through the five steps of engagement. Only then will you be able to define the ideal experience and, just as importantly, only then will you have the means to measure and optimize your offer.

5
Commitment 5: Measure and Optimize

Many men will, we think, recognize the following situation. You're getting ready to go out when your wife or partner comes up to you with two dresses in her hand to ask which one you think is the best. For you, this is an irrelevant question because you know that the way you feel about her has nothing to do with the dress she chooses.

However what we are trying to get at here is that when you ask a loved one a question, you have to make it a relevant question! (It may be worth noting, in passing, what psychologists believe about the dress question. They suggest that your wife or partner is not asking you to choose her dress, since she already knows you do not have the right taste. What she is really trying to do is have a conversation with you. So next time, just say, "Both look good on you", and start a conversation.)

How does this relate to design? In this way: towards the end of the design phase, it is common to organize various tests for such touchpoints as products, online environments and packaging. We have however sometimes been involved in and experienced a number of ineffective tests that wasted resources and money for the company by asking irrelevant questions. And we have, over a number of years, generated considerable knowledge about conducting effective design tests.

If you are a CEO of a company you will naturally want to be as certain as you can that your new launches will be both successful in the short term and build the brand for the longer term, by using the "right measurement" to grow the business – and at the same time set clear KPIs and governance. We'd like to share that experience with you in the rest of this chapter. What follow are some tips for effective touchpoint design tests.

KNOW WHAT YOU WANT TO ACHIEVE

What we mean by this is that you should always determine the key function and achievements you want from the particular touchpoint. Let's take packaging as an example. If you want to test a packaging design, ask yourself what you want to achieve by maximizing the value of the packaging touchpoint.

Packaging has been called the "silent sales assistant" because it is a very powerful sales tool in the retail environment. So, if packaging *is* your sales assistant, what would you like it to achieve in a retail environment? We assume you would want it to 1) capture the attention of your audiences, and then 2) very clearly communicate a unique and distinctive proposition to them. And we think it's fair to say you would also want it to 3) behave and act according to your brand values and beliefs. (Note that this all corresponds to the stages you went through when you met your partner, as described in the Introduction.)

So if this is what you want your packaging to achieve then you should only set three goals for the design test of a packaging touchpoint. You want to know whether it:

• Stands out

• Encourages customers to purchase the product

• Fits with your brand positioning.

We sometimes ask questions with no relevance to the goal of the touchpoint. For example, asking "Which colour do you like?" or "Do you consider this colour innovative?" is, we believe, irrelevant when evaluating the performance and design of packaging. You should always keep the questions relevant.

(And it is, by the way, useful to limit your questions to a minimum. When people know it will cost just the same to ask more questions they tend to add more to the test. But most of the time, the extra questions add nothing relevant and usually end up confusing you more than helping you.)

KNOW WHAT ROLE YOU WANT THE TOUCHPOINT TO PERFORM

When you test a touchpoint – such as product, online or user interface – you should always be clear about the role you want it to fulfil. In general, there are two roles for each touchpoint.

- **Role 1** – to attract and persuade your audiences by communicating your unique proposition, a proposition based on your brand values and beliefs

- **Role 2** – to keep engaging and delighting your audiences during the five stages of experience (see Chapter 4 for a description of each stage), and to do so based on your brand values and beliefs.

Testing role 1

Start by asking the same three questions listed already (regardless of the touchpoint). Does it:

1. **Stand out?** Can you get the attention of your audiences?

2. **Encourage customers to purchase the product and/or service?** Can you describe your "unique" proposition with a relevant and meaningful claim?

3. **Fit with your brand positioning?** Have you remained
   authentic to your brand values and beliefs?

Throughout our careers, we have participated in a number
of so-called "face value tests". During such tests, a company usually compares a new concept design with a competitor's design by asking people which one's looks they
prefer. Although we agree that, in the end, your product
will be displayed next to your competitor's on a retail shelf
and will need to be liked by your audiences, we always
think this type of test only works when you do *not* have a
unique proposition. If your proposition is the same as, or
very close to, your competitor's, then all you are really
engaging in is a beauty contest. And if you *are* in this situation, then let's hope that your product has the better
"looks" and can sell more than similar products on the
same shelf.

However, if you *do* have a unique proposition, one of the
most important functions of a touchpoint such as product
design is that it expresses the proposition and radiates the
values of your brand to your audiences in a retail environment. Therefore what you want to know from the test is
this: *which concept will generate interest in, and communicate most about, your unique proposition?* For example,
if you are the first to market with a unique proposition
such as the Senseo coffee maker from Philips, there is no
reason for you to compare the looks of the product design
with other drip type coffee makers from competitors.

Testing role 2

To test role 2 you can, as we mentioned in Chapter 4, use
the discovery and use stages of the five engagement stages.
   To test the *discovery* stage, you should organize various
sessions with your early experience demonstrator to

check that your interaction is intuitive, as well as easy to start up and become familiar with. The types of questions you should ask are fully described in Chapter 9, in the section about the *Attractive* attribute. They include:

- Is your proposition easy-to-use, with intuitive interaction (either already known or easy to learn)?

- Does it minimize the user's effort by removing unnecessary complexity?

- Does it enable immediate use and invite further exploration, offering relevant choices when needed?

- Is it easily recognized, understood and remembered with a minimum of conscious effort?

When you test the *use* stage you should organize an extended survey so that you can monitor changes in people's judgement regarding your proposition and its usability. This is very useful feedback for your user or customer journey mapping, as it enables you to identify:

1. Frequently used functions that either satisfy ("Every time I close the door of my Mercedes, the sound it makes confirms the quality of the whole car") or disturb ("Every time I squeeze oranges, it is annoying to have to clean all the parts of the machine by hand").

2. Surprising elements that confirm satisfaction with use. ("The other day I was visiting a town I am not familiar with. I had the address of a place I needed to visit in an email on my iPhone. When I accidentally touched the address, the iPhone automatically opened the Map application, to show both my current position and the location I needed to reach".)

The type of questions you can ask are:

- Does it engage all relevant senses (lighting effect), sound quality, scent and tactile interaction, etc.) and maximize their pleasure in use?

- Have you improved usability from the previous propositions?

TAKE MEASUREMENTS OVER A NUMBER OF YEARS

The benefit of this is that you are not only able to compare your performance over several years, but can also accumulate knowledge about how to resolve or improve a design when faced with negative results. People faced with a bad performance result who do not have fixed measurements tend to panic and re-start the entire design from scratch without actually knowing how to fix the problem(s). With accumulated knowledge, it's possible to fine-tune work instead of re-doing it all.

For example, in Philips, we once saw that the performance of the three measurements already listed – *stands out in a retail environment*; *encourages customers to purchase the product and/or service*; and *fits with your brand positioning* – were dramatically improved by changing lifestyle images to detailed shots of the product proposition, or by simply changing the background colour of photographs for different countries. In each case our past experiences made us able to apply simple improvements systematically instead of blindly trying to re-design the entire packaging design. (In most cases, re-design means just changing layout, which does not offer any improvements.)

CHOOSE A NUMBER OF MEASUREMENTS TO ACHIEVE BALANCE

You should always use balanced measurements to achieve your goal. At one point in his book *Buyology*, Martin Lindstrom examined the effectiveness of applying sexual images to communications. Referring to a study in which the image of a beautiful, half-naked female model had been tested with male audiences, he noted that eye-tracking tests had revealed that most of the time the viewers' eyes had stayed in one place: on the model's breasts. The test results also showed that only 9.8% of the viewers remembered the brand and proposition of the communication in which the model had been used. Lindstrom calls this the "vampire effect". This is why we believe it is not that difficult to fulfil one purpose with your touchpoint, but is a challenge to fulfil several at the same time.

Fulfilling only one measurement out of the three listed at the beginning of this chapter is easier than trying to fulfil them all at once. For example, if you were to apply sexual images to your test, you would most likely manage to improve the *stands out in a retail environment* measurement (although even that might be a challenge given that the media are so full of sexual images these days) than trying to fulfil all three of them at the same time.

LISTEN, LEARN AND RESPOND

We have also learned that it is very useful to plan several tests (we recommend three) so that you can learn from, and respond to, any unexpected delays and setbacks. Doing this provides you with the pre-planned time to react to potentially negative feedback and improve your performance in a structured manner. That's why we strongly recommend installing a "listen, learn and respond" methodology in your design tests: to avoid any panicked reactions.

It's been our experience that companies quite often squeeze the test schedule into their production plan, even though they have no time to wait for the first result. If this is the case, then the purpose of the test is not to learn from the market – and so get closer to the audiences by providing better propositions; rather, it's to create an internal excuse when the proposition fails in the market. That's why, to realize "listen, learn and respond", it is crucial that you formally integrate it into your company business creation and/or product creation process. You should, obviously, also determine the most effective timing so that you can use the methodology to maximize what you learn about each touchpoint.

DON'T FORGET THE PURPOSE OF YOUR DESIGN TEST

Organizing a series of touchpoint tests is costly in terms of both time and resources. So if you are going to apply a test you should make sure of its ROI. To do this, you should never forget that the purpose of such tests is to learn about, and improve, your design execution so that you make your business a success.

But note that the touchpoint test is different from a test of your proposition. Testing a proposition needs to occur *before* you start the design process of your touchpoints. (It should happen during the proposition and direction step. See Chapter 11 for more about this.) In one such packaging test we participated in, we discovered that the proposition itself was wrong rather than the design execution. For this reason we would say that if you want to test your proposition you should test the full touchpoint experience with your unique proposition during the proposition and direction phase.

It's been our experience on many occasions that people get upset and then panic when confronted with negative results for touchpoint tests. Yet most of the time, when they start to examine the content of the tests, they cannot find the actual causes of the poor results: which means that their organization is left with negative results and no clue as to how to resolve the problem. The truth is that you actually do not know whether you can rely on the result of this test or any other. The only way to avoid wasting your organization's time and resources is to provide a firm and solid structure for all the tests you want to carry out.

In short, know what you want to measure, work out the best way to do it, and then stick to your methodology.

6

Commitment 6: Introduce a "Love Tester"

Many years ago, Nintendo brought out a toy intended to measure the level of love. Because Yasushi could only vaguely remember it, he surfed the internet while writing this book and found it in the beforemario blog (at: http://blog.beforemario.com/2011/02/nintendo-love-tester-1969.html). It was explained as follows:

> To use the toy, a couple would hold hands with one another while holding one of the two metal cups each. The meter in the Love Tester would then indicate the "level of love" that existed between the couple, using a scale of 0 to 100.

It was indeed the toy Yasushi remembered! And while we don't think you need to test the level of your love for your audiences on a scale of 0 to 100, we do believe it needs to be unconditional and that it is useful to know how to use tangible indicators to measure it effectively.

Therefore as a leader of your company, as part of your research methodology, it helps to have clear performance measurements to evaluate your brand, your design performance and its contribution to building a loved brand (by linking it with business success and growth). That said

however it should be noted that this is a challenging subject, which a number of organizations have already
addressed.

For example, in 2007, the Design Council of London
produced the *Value of Design Fact Finder Report*. It was
based on two pieces of Design Council research conducted
in 2005 and 2006. One looked at how businesses use and
understand design, and at how it impacts their performance. The other studied the way in which businesses add
value to their offer, how they use design to do so and how
this impacts on performance. The report offered the following striking facts:

- Every £100 that a design-conscious business spends on
  design increases turnover by £225

- In businesses where design is integral to operations, over
  three quarters say they've increased their competitive-
  ness and turnover because of design

- Shares in design-led businesses outperform key stock
  market indices by 200%

- On average, design-conscious businesses increase their
  market share by 6.3%.

These findings illustrate why, for us, it is useful for the
design function to set up clear performance measurements
that could 1) indicate a link between the contribution of
design and the brand/company performance, and 2) be
used to review, monitor and – potentially – provide tips to
improve their performance.

We have had experience of two such design performance
measurements and would like to offer some brief thoughts
on both. One comes from using the Net Promoter Score
(NPS), which illuminates the link between business growth
and design's contribution, and can be used to review,

monitor and possibly improve the performance of both. The other comes from winning design awards, which we admit offers no clear link between business growth and design's contribution, nor ways of improving them. However what it *does* do is provide a clear indication of design's performance among leaders and peers.

USING THE NPS

For those not familiar with NPS, it is a customer loyalty metric developed by Fred Reichheld, Bain & Company and Satmetrix, and introduced in the book *The Ultimate Question* (Reichheld, 2009). It suggests that the answer to one question – "How likely is it that you would recommend our company to a friend or colleague?" – has a correlation with company results and therefore its growth.

If NPS data do indeed have a correlation with company growth, then we can use these data to see how directly design-related aspects contribute. By understanding this, we can also evaluate and monitor the effectiveness of the design function's contribution to the company performance. Therefore we investigated how to utilize NPS data to evaluate how well design contributes to NPS, and how we can contribute further to improving NPS scores with the help of experts in Philips.

Measuring performance

To measure design performance with NPS, you need to install a mechanism to ask people the reason for their judgement when you also ask them to give a rating on a NPS scale of zero to ten. You can record the feedback with spontaneous reactions, and also by showing prefixed root causes – that you prepare – specific to your industry or product category.

Based on the feedback of both spontaneous and guided root causes, you can identify the feedback related to both aesthetic and functional aspects (for example, ease of set up, installation and use) as "design drivers for impact". (See Chapter 9 for more about design drivers.) By investigating these aspects under promoters, passives and detractors you can then identify the influence of both aspects against the total NPS score.

Evaluating performance

When you've collected all the data, you can evaluate your specific performance against design drivers in your industry or category. You can also compare your design drivers against the NPS leader and your main competitors (not to mention gaining fresh insight into the difference between various industries and countries). We also believe that you can, potentially, map the root causes in your customer journey and contextualize the issues raised in the project.

Furthermore if you can identify a direct relationship in the financial growth prediction with a specific NPS distractor point, you can then calculate the internal investment required to improve specific NPS distractor scores. You can calculate them against the predictions of growth for your business (complete ROI) based on your NPS insights.

Should you decide to use NPS to collect data, remember that it's also very important to continue to use for accumulating data over several years. By doing that you will be able to analyse trends in specific countries. (For example, Chinese people are, in general, extremely brand conscious. In most categories they rate brands as one of the main reasons for recommending it to others.)

You can also use the data to follow changes in a specific category. To offer an example: it has been noted that people's awareness of design in a category has been seen to change both before and after a single brand proposition. Therefore it is interesting to observe this not only to understand each market, but also to understand how markets might react when an entirely new brand or proposition breaks current category codes.

WINNING DESIGN AWARDS

In 2008 and 2009, we worked on an awards strategy. As you know, there are a number of design-related awards in the world. Some of them are well known globally, while others are more locally focused. Winning any of these types of award is another valid way of measuring your design quality and ability against that of your peers. And, as we wrote at the beginning of this chapter, although we must admit that there is (as yet) no proven correlation between winning design awards and building a loved brand, or business success and growth, winning design awards *does* have a number of obvious merits for your brand, your company and increasing your design leadership. For example, awards can help to:

- Build brand equity
- Protect you against imitation (visibility and claiming leadership)
- Assert your design credentials through PR and publicity
- Call attention (public and media) to specific products, services or capabilities
- Earn employee attention, motivation and praise
- Attract and retain new talent and clients
- Communicate both your status as an "A-list firm" and your ability to innovate

- Gain the public's confidence, trust and preference over competitors (with marketing)
- Win a seal of approval (measure of quality) for your products and services
- Enjoy the benefit of the award value itself (money, rights or privileges).

With that said, we would now like to suggest a few ways to make the winning of awards part of your design function's strategy.

SOME TIPS FOR WINNING AWARDS

One essential requirement for winning design awards is to possess strong, unique, distinctive and high quality design concepts that you can submit to the various awards bodies. Producing the concepts in the first place is not easy – we would hope that the High Design approach provides tips about that – but what we *can* share with you are some of our own experiences about how to maximize your assets to win awards. (And it is worth noting that entering concepts for design awards will mean both internal costs – preparation and submission of documentation, etc. – and external cost – such as transportation and participation fees. For that reason, it might at first be worth your while to consider how you could win more with a limited effort.)

Once, at Philips, we were attached to a team responsible for winning design awards. In 2008 we raised our annual target on the "hit rate" (the ratio of submissions to the number of wins) and the "absolute number of awards actually won". And year after year we increased our performance by introducing new ways of working. Our absolute number of wins increased more than 60% over four years.

What follows are a few tips for participating in design awards competitions.

Create an award calendar

There are so many design awards throughout the world that it is obviously not realistic to participate in all of them. Therefore the first thing you need to do is select the criteria you will use to choose the awards you value most. These might, for example, include:

- International prominence in your key trading regions, and in the locations where your design talent is based
- Support for a specific category or business need
- Suitability of the competition to your company or business strategy (for example, sustainability)
- Suitability of the competition to your core capabilities (but without ruling out new competitions should your company come up with new capabilities)
- A balance between competitions recognized by professionals or peers and competitions recognized by consumers
- Competitions offering an established and credible judge of your brand and propositions
- Competitions that attract the top 500 companies or brands
- Prestige and level of recognition
- Amount or range of publicity resulting from the award.

Remember that your criteria should be based on the benefits you want to gain by winning awards. When you have chosen them, you should then select all the awards you plan to participate in annually. You should also arrange quarterly meetings to review the list. These will enable you to add any newly discovered or introduced awards.

When you have done this, it is vital that you make one global award calendar. This will help you to prepare all your submissions – on time – for all the awards you have chosen and to share that information throughout your company.

Build up your knowledge about the awards selected

It is useful to build up insights about the awards that you select. Information on winning categories and brands over the years will give you some idea of each award's specific character and the focus of the judges. These insights will help you choose the most "suitable" concepts for each particular award.

Make an internal selection first

To avoid filling in separate award templates for each submission, the designers at Philips created one internal template for every designer to fill in just once. We then used the information we gathered from this to make one "central" submission for the various awards. (You can also use such a template to set up a simple quarterly time frame for internal submissions.) Once you have done this, you can then choose the most promising concepts to send to the awards based on such criteria as:

Balanced "portfolio"

- Capability spread: balance between your various capabilities

- Stakeholder spread: balance between awards recognized by professionals/peers and consumer awards

Business fit

- Is the submission a good representation of the brand?

- Does it support a business strategy or a strong local category or need?

Probability of success

- How well does the submission meet with insights about the targeted awards?
- Is this a new proposition in a market?
- Does it suggest a new approach?

Design quality

- Look and feel
- Interaction or messaging structure.

Instantly grab attention by sharpening your story

This may sound rather obvious, but you need to have a clear and sharp story to show why your concept is superior to others. If you have ever been a juror in one of these awards competitions, you probably already know this; for those who haven't, it's vital to remember that all the jurors need to make their decisions in a very limited time. So that makes it essential for you to make a clear and sharp claim on their attention. (Although we said at the beginning that this was obvious, we should note that for some designers it is not a common practice.)

You may also find that you need to challenge your designers to provide you with just such a clear and sharp claim for their concepts – based on your proposition framework. (See Chapter 12 for more about this.) It is also helpful to ask copywriters and communication strategists to study the resulting descriptions, to see whether they can sharpen and clarify them even further.

FIND THE RIGHT MEASUREMENT FOR YOUR BRAND

These are the two measurements we have experience with. But there are others you can use when evaluating your brand, a design's performance and its contribution to building a loved brand. (For example, *Best Global Brand Ranking from Interbrand* and *Design Value* by Peter Zec and Burkhard Jacob (2010).) But the most important point we want to share with you in this section is that you need to find the right measurements for your purpose and then apply them constantly. That way, you will always have tangible results when reviewing, monitoring and improving your performance.

Part 3

Know What You Will Bring Your Audience

7

Commitment 7: Build a Clear Brand Design Architecture

When your old printer is broken and you need to buy a new one, what do you do? We imagine that, like most people, you simply think about the few brands you associate with printers – such as HP, Epson and Canon – and visit their home pages to start searching for the new one?

MANY BRANDS, MANY PROPOSITIONS

When you look at your brand from your end-user's and customer's (outside-in) perspective, what you often see is just one of many brands and many products and service offers – nothing else. Yet people usually understand these offers under existing marketing categories. This means that people project your portfolios into existing marketing categories and categorize your brand within those categories. For example, if your brand offers a kitchen blender, people associate your brand with the kitchen appliances category. If your brand offers financial services, people associate your brand with the financial market category. That's why brand associations with your targeted market categories are so important for your brand, since you want it to be the brand at the top of people's minds within the market categories you are active in. If it is, people will think about your brand first when they need to purchase a product and/or services in your market category.

That's why, to achieve strong associations with your brand and market category, you should carefully manage and monitor the number of your offerings in that market. In their book *The 22 Immutable Laws of Branding*, Al Ries and Laura Ries (1998) state – under "The Law of Expansion" – that:

> While extending the line might bring added sales in the short term, it runs counter to the notion of branding. If you want to build a powerful brand in the minds of consumers, you need to contract your brand, not expand it. In the long term, expanding your brand will diminish your power and weaken your image.

As Ries and Ries point out, your brand image and association is stronger if you have fewer propositions in your market. This is a point of view we strongly agree with: in general, when a brand has a too wide and insufficiently clustered product and/or service portfolio, people may lose a clear association with it: therefore it will be harder to maintain a strong brand image and association. Of course there are exceptions to this law; one notable example that springs to mind is Virgin. But, in general, it is only when your brand value is clearly and authentically articulated through all market categories that you can manage to maintain a widely spread portfolio. You must always balance the strength of your brand value in people's minds against the breadth of your portfolio.

A CLEAR BRAND ARCHITECTURE

A dilemma facing any successful brand is finding the balance between extending a product range to build and grow

its business and maintaining a strong brand image and
association. For us, the only way to do this is to build a
clear brand architecture. And to do that you need to cluster your range of products into higher-level propositions.
This will result in your brand story remaining strong while
also offering you the opportunity to expand your product
and service offers within your market. The main purpose
of a brand architecture is to offer brand product and service propositions to the market in a clear, consistent structure from an outside-in point of view.

(Responsibility for the brand architecture should be
assumed by a brand manager – a role we believe should
very much belong to the CEO of a brand, as described in
Chapter 1. And it will be the job of a brand manager to
create a structure that delivers strong but effective market
messages. A brand architecture should *not* relate to organizational structure.)

We would argue that a brand should give guidance to
users and customers by acting like a light-house. As Stefano
Marzano said in his keynote speech, "Driving Innovation
in Corporate Culture": "The brand is that lighthouse, and
in theory the company behind the brand can make the
light that comes from it as bright as it wants through advertising and PR. But ultimately the offer has to be credible."
If that is so, then a brand must create a clear structure to
guide its credible and unique offer. Therefore your brand
architecture should be constructed fully from an outside-in
point of view, because its purpose is to guide people clearly
through the unique propositions you intend to offer.

People will use this type of architecture to understand
and navigate a brand, in much the same way as they
approach a shop. People choose which shop to enter based
on the industry and the brand's promise (for example, a
supermarket might offer a promise of a specific range, selection and/or quality). A supermarket divides its floor plan
into departments (domains) that are easily understood and

recognized by the customers (food, clothing, household goods, etc.). Within these departments, there are categories (the food department will offer meat, fish, cereals, etc.). The shop is arranged in an outside-in perspective so that customers can easily navigate it and find the value on offer.

WHAT DO WE MEAN BY "BRAND ARCHITECTURE" AND "BRAND"?

Many writers refer to what we call the "branding approach" as brand architecture. For us, though, brand architecture refers to the way in which you structure your brand – with your value proposition positioned inside an operational domain and category – to make your brand story clear and therefore accessible to your audiences. We see the branding approach as something a company needs to choose based on its marketing strategy. It is indeed a starting point when building a brand but we think it's misleading to call it a brand architecture.

Before we touch on different types of branding approach, we think it would be best to clarify what we mean by a brand. For us, a brand is something with a recognized name and value – Audi, iPod or Vaio – and not the name of a company. Furthermore, we believe it is up to the end-users and customers to decide what a brand is and what it is not. We believe this more accurately reflects the reality of brands in the market, for we are sure there are many brands that were born more as the result of market recognition than a company's intentions. A brand exists in the minds of its customers and it may take on a life of its own or disappear entirely from their consciousness. For us, a brand is what people feel it is.

Therefore it is very important for your company to nurture the brand – and to ensure that it is recognized appropriately – by monitoring the gap between your intentions and market perception and recognition. And based on your data, business scope, strategy and legacy, as well as the outside-in view of how customers navigate the category, domain and market, you can then create different types of branding approach.

THREE TYPES OF BRANDING APPROACH

Various texts describe several branding approaches, but we have found the following three to be the simplest, whilst still fulfilling all business needs:

- Monolithic
- Endorsed
- Stand alone.

Monolithic – corporate or umbrella brands

These are consumer-facing brands used across all the firm's activities. The name, monolithic, is how it is known to all of its stakeholders; for example, IBM, Philips and Apple. These brands may also be used in conjunction with product descriptions or sub-brands.

Endorsed – endorsed brands and sub-brands

These brands include a brand as an endorsement. The endorsing brand is often a corporate or umbrella brand, or a family brand. The endorsement should add credibility to the endorsed sub-brand in the eyes of consumers. For example, Nestlé's Kit Kat or Ralph Lauren's Polo.

Stand alone – individual product brands

Individual brands are presented to consumers, often without them being aware of the parent company name. (Nor does the parent company promote such brands.) Other stakeholders however, such as shareholders or partners, will know the producer by its company name; for example, Procter & Gamble's Pampers or Unilever's Dove brands. (It's worth noting that Unilever and Procter & Gamble are now utilizing their corporate brands as an endorser in some markets – deliberately so. We assume they have realized that customers will try other products by them because their company's name has given those products credibility: which also, of course, builds value in the "corporate" brand.)

CHOOSING A BRANDING APPROACH

From time to time, each company adapts its direction based on people's subjective perception of its assets in the market. It does this to effectively leverage and grow its assets by communicating its proposition within a dynamic market environment.

Therefore the most important factors to consider when choosing a branding approach are as follows:

1. Understand your assets (recognition, value, etc. in the market).

2. Understand your organizational capacity (resources for communicating various assets, as well as the disciplines and principles required to realize and maintain complex brand and portfolio management).

3. Create your strategy from an outside-in point of view.

4. Thoroughly deploy – and stick to – your strategy and governance model. (Some companies quite often make a rule and then start to make exceptions. But such small holes in the 'dam' will, eventually, break the entire plan of a brand.)

THE BRAND ARCHITECTURE

If you agree that the most important message you want to reach your audiences is about your brand value and your belief in your product and service, then we propose expressing your brand architecture as shown in Figure 7.1.

Each of the circles in Figure 7.1 represents a specific facet of the brand's structure, as described here.

The **brand** circle contains the brand's values, beliefs and personality, as discussed in Chapter 1.

The **domain** circle contains the domains – as seen by the customers – in which the brand operates; for example, consumer electronics, automobile, insurance or health care. Obviously, if your brand operates within one domain, this is an implicit circle for it (although it is important for your brand to be aware of the fact). Regardless of whether you have one single domain or multiple domains, you need to

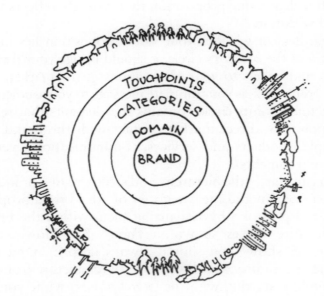

Figure 7.1 *Brand architecture circles*

make a clear decision about whether your core value proposition lies in the *domain* circle or the *category* circle. If you decide to place your value proposition in the *domain* circle, then you should create a single, strong value proposition that clearly reflects your brand.

It is common, for example, for automotive companies to create their value proposition in the *domain* circle because they rarely cross over into another domain. By contrast, Virgin is an often-cited example of a rare brand that successfully takes its brand into many domains, installing a high-level proposition in each domain that strongly bridges from its brand values and beliefs.

The **category** circle contains the products or services – as seen by the customers – offered by the brand within each domain. For example, home entertainment, personal entertainment and gaming are typical categories within the consumer electronics domain. If you do not have one overall value proposition in the *domain* circle, then you should install a clear value proposition that strongly reflects your brand within it.

Regardless of whether your value proposition lies in the *domain* or the *category* circle, it should bridge your (brand) values and beliefs to your propositions in the market. The value proposition is your ultimate message to your audiences.

The **touchpoints** circle contains the elements that represent points of direct market contact with the brand (for example, products and services, communications, people and environments).

You can clarify the hierarchy and structure of a brand, its market domain and the categories of your brand propositions and portfolio by visualizing them within the Brand Architecture circles shown in Figure 7.1. However as Figure 7.2 shows you should always keep in mind that your target audiences will view your architecture from the outside-in – starting with the (*touchpoints*) while you see things from the inside-out (starting with the *brand*).

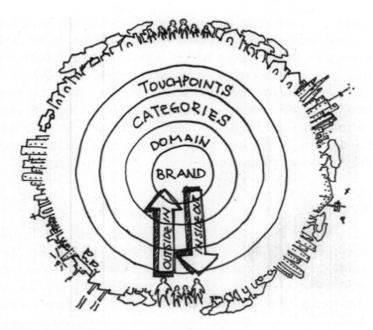

Figure 7.2 *Different perspectives*

Therefore what you need to construct is a clear architecture that enables you to:

1. Communicate your brand values and beliefs to your audiences so effectively that you add credibility to your offer in the market.

2. Cluster your range of products into higher-level propositions and make sure your brand is strongly associated with those propositions.

BRAND DESIGN ARCHITECTURE

Brand design architecture is one of the strategic elements a brand needs to manifest its brand architecture into a clear – and total – brand experience. Here, design can be best described as the articulation of the brand through visualization and interaction based on the brand's values, beliefs and personality. By applying a well-structured design identity system, you can "orchestrate" a brand experience across a company portfolio, one that will reflect and communicate your intended brand promise and the value proposition of your portfolio. We call this design identity system the brand design architecture (BDA). It reflects the brand architecture structure and descriptions at each level (as shown in Figure 7.1).

Brand

This circle contains the brand design identity principle (reflecting the brand's values, beliefs and personality. See Chapter 10.) It also contains the brand level assets (company logo, name, colour, etc.). It is the fundamental core of the brand and a brand's creative director needs to ensure that its behaviours (manner) and appearance (wardrobe) occur throughout the brand. It is very important that the content be well understood (not only by the design function, but also by all the other functions in the company) and well respected. For this reason it is vital to install the mechanism for continuous training and support (including IT tools).

Domain

Regardless of whether your brand has one or more domains, if you have a value proposition in the *domain* circle, then you should also create an identity in the *domain* circle.

Design should articulate and manifest the value proposition through visualization and interaction by reflecting the brand's values, beliefs and personality. Therefore you should install a well-structured design identity system where you have your value proposition.

Category

When your brand has a value proposition in the *category* circle, you should also install an identity in the *category* circle.

We believe that an identity should always be coupled with a value proposition. Theoretically you could create an unlimited number of identities, just as long as each identity followed your brand identity policy – although, as Ries and Ries state under The Law of Expansion in their book *The 22 Immutable Laws of Branding*, we cannot believe a brand exists that could manage to create and maintain a strong brand image and an association with an unlimited number of propositions: something that would lead to unlimited unique identities.

Touchpoints

The *touchpoints* circle contains the articulation of either the domain or category identity; for example, the translation of an overall domain identity into a website design identity.

Another case study from the Design Council's Design Leadership Programme website is World First, a foreign exchange company that Neil coached himself.

World First is the UK's fastest-growing foreign exchange company. Launched in 2004 by managing directors Jonathan Quin and Nick Robinson, the London-based business is committed to building fair and transparent long-term relationships with its clients and prides itself on providing every one of its customers with a quality, personal service. It is valued by its customers for being quick, efficient and friendly.

The company has established a strong position in its marketplace by promising better exchange rates than most high street banks, better service with all transactions completed effectively, and better advice – on exchange rate volatility, for example, to ensure the right transaction is made at the right rate at the right time. Since launch it has worked with more than 29,000 private clients and almost 8500 companies and has developed a number of service innovations including an online trading platform, a mobile app and a way to connect directly to its clients' systems to automate their payments.

Problem

In early 2010 World First's management team sought external help from the Design Council's Design Leadership Programme (called Designing Demand at the time), which offers independent direction and guidance to small and medium sized private and public sector enterprises enabling them to use design to grow through becoming more innovative, more competitive and more profitable.

The first step for World First was to participate in a workshop at which external design advisors discussed different aspects of the business. This event was co-ordinated and facilitated by Neil who briefed the external design advisers on what to review. Looking back, Quin now describes this as "a break through moment" for his company. "The feeling was our identity was bland and indistinctive", he says. "We realized we had a design in the sense we had a logo, but without a clear tone of voice and consistent framework for visual and verbal references about ourselves, we didn't have a brand."

Neil knew that the approach needed for brand communication at launch was no longer the approach they should be using six years down the line. A more strategic design approach was required. Strategic design is underpinned by deep insight and a clear understanding of the wider, business, market and customer context. When used in this way, design is more than a new logo and can deliver real business value.

The company's identity in its early years was deliberately more corporate to gain customers' confidence, but it wasn't doing justice to the values of the company and its customer-focused, personal approach. This was also against a backdrop of anti-corporate bank zeitgeist with the global crash, which meant their values were even more important to communicate through their brand design architecture.

The management team decided to invest in a strategic re-branding project before attempting to re-design any key touchpoints.

The first step was to undertake further research into World First's business by conducting in-depth interviews with senior staff and key clients to better understand the company and the business environment in which it operates. Work had already begun internally to try to define the business's values. Designers worked closely with the management team to help them further refine this. This process resulted in a hierarchy of themes from which a streamlined set of values relating to what the business should stand for were agreed.

The team encapsulated this thinking in a simple phrase: "On your side"; because of how highly World First values its relationships with customers and how this, in turn, shapes the services it provides and distinguishes them from their competition.

"On your side" was an idea inspired by the company's customers. It is an idea that's true to what the business does, how it works and how it is perceived.

Attention then moved to how this idea could be articulated and visualized. The designers presented a number of different styles of approach. The one chosen is fresh and modern, incorporating the "On your side" line into the company logo, which also features an upright coloured bar to the left of the company name – a visual symbol to convey a dividing line between World First and its competitors.

The brand design had to be distinctive and also flexible, as the business had ambitious growth plans. It needed to work across a wide range of communications channels and touchpoints too – online, in print and at events, as well as on coffee cups and even podcasts. A fresh emphasis was placed on photography across its branded communications featuring the company's staff.

Another important aspect was finding the right tone of voice for the company to use when speaking about itself, because the staff members were a key touchpoint of the brand. All key players within the company were involved throughout the project because it's so much easier to get everyone to buy into the final result when they've been personally involved along the way.

Impact

World First's new branding was first launched internally in autumn 2010, and well received. An external launch in November that same year was then supported by a PR and marketing campaign.

Monitoring of the website meanwhile showed no dips in the number of visitors – which can happen when a site is re-launched. In fact over the weeks that followed all the stats – number of visits, pages viewed, time spent on the site and so on – rose. Average time spent on the site, for example, rose 70% from the level before the re-design.

Previously World First had had little to say about itself and what set it apart, other than what it did and what services it provided. Since the re-branding however every employee is now able to not only talk about what the company does but who it is and what it stands for – putting people first – which permeates everything the business does, and provides a strong springboard for conversation with potential customers.

In the year following the re-branding the volume of media appearances by company staff rose significantly. In the year before the re-launch World First featured in 54 items of press coverage; in the three month post, this figure was 133.

Quin believes World First's investment in branding contributed directly towards the 31% growth the company enjoyed in 2011 (during a deep recession). It has also helped the business when hiring to attract and better retain the best people.

Thanks to the Design Council's programme, we moved on from thinking that "logo = brand" to understanding that our brand permeates everything we do and includes, for example, the tone of voice of communication, customer experience and the design of our offices. We also expanded our view of design; from just thinking about graphic design to thinking about design in its

> widest context. For example, we went through
> every customer touch point and objectively
> assessed each from a strategic design perspective
> to work out how to improve them. Your brand
> becomes what you stand for as a business and
> understanding and living your brand in every-
> thing you do adds real value to your company.
> ...
> Knowing what you stand for as a business and
> communicating it effectively in everything you
> do adds real value to your company.
>
> World First Co-Founder, Jonathan Quin

THE ULTIMATE GOAL OF A BRAND DESIGN ARCHITECTURE

The ultimate goal of a brand design architecture is to communicate your brand values and beliefs to your audience,
making your propositions with the aid of touchpoints. We
believe it will help you do this by bringing an outside-in
perspective to your company, enabling you to clarify your
brand story and, in turn, apply design in the most effective
manner.

Ultimately, a brand wants to engage with people about
its brand values and beliefs – but it also wants to move
beyond its current category and touchpoints. For example,
in the 1990s, during the early phases of the mobile phone
category, many people saw Sony as one of the top mobile
phone brands. However, at that time, Sony had not yet
entered the mobile phone domain. For me, it was a time
when Sony's values and beliefs were still strongly engaged
with its public, with values and beliefs that came from
founder Masaru Ibuka. He wanted, he said, "To establish

an ideal factory that stresses a spirit of freedom and open-mindedness, and where engineers with sincere motivation can exercise their technological skills to the highest level." (Is it only us who believes this also resembles the Apple promise to *think different*?)

When people are fully engaged with your brand, and fully understand and recognize you through your values and beliefs, then they will expect you to be a leader in all categories that match and reflect those values and beliefs.

8
Commitment 8: Continuously Innovate

For a brand to ensure and maintain its long-term sustainability, we believe it needs to continuously innovate. And that's why we think it's interesting to study some key findings from the Brand Innovation 2000 study, conducted by Profit Impact of Market Strategy (PIMS), with assistance from IMD for the European Brand Association – and offering evidence from 35 of Europe's key brand builders (including Bacardi/Martini, Douwe Egberts, Electrolux, Kimberly Clark, Mars, Nestle, Philips, P&G and Unilever). What follows are some of the study's findings.

- Strong brands are built on innovations – usually radical innovations that create real consumer value – not just good advertising and promotion.

- Radical innovations that enhance consumer value drive higher growth in market share and sales than a series of incremental improvements.

- Pioneer brands – the ultimate radical innovators – enjoy years of benefits. Getting to market first with a defensible advantage is what most "big winners" do.

- Successful innovations focus on consumer value right from the start.

- Speed to markets is a major factor in growing sales and market share.

- Successful innovators who also improve the consumer's perception of their brand reduce their costs of communicating the next new launch.

- Testing the marketing approach itself is useful. Brands with value adding innovation can still fail from poor marketing and communication.

It was clear from the study that all 35 companies clearly recognized and agreed on the advantages offered by the continuous innovation of a brand. So what actual challenges does innovation – and related activities – pose to a brand and a company? That is the subject of this chapter.

THE CHALLENGE OF HANDLING INNOVATION AND OPERATIONS

Although the importance of continuous innovation is clearly recognized and understood by a number of companies, it is still challenging for any organization to handle "innovation" while also maintaining "operational excellence" in today's market. So it's important to consciously recognize the difference between the two.

Imagine, for example, that you've decided to install a new transportation infrastructure in a city. Your "innovation" will consist of choosing the right transportation – such as a train system – and then developing stations and routes for railways and roads. For you, the most important elements in such innovation would be a clear vision of how to contribute to society and how best to shape the city of the future for the happiness and prosperity of its inhabitants. Therefore all the actions you take should be based on your understanding of the short- and long-term needs of people and society.

Conversely, your "operational excellence" will come from maintaining stations and running trains on the installed railways and roads in the most effective and efficient manner to maximize the value of the assets. (In a slight deviation from the topic, we would like to point out that most Japanese train companies operate with extreme efficiency. We have always thought that the Japanese should not just export their products, but also their know-how about such topics.)

As you can easily see, these two activities require a different culture, mentality, talents and ways of working. Yet several times over the years we have observed how an organization (unconsciously) applies a short-term business approach to long-term innovation projects or programmes. We've also encountered companies trying to hold on to an existing operational infrastructure regardless of new and innovative approaches. This does not benefit a company. In fact, we would go so far as to say that the existing operational infrastructure on which the original offerings and business model were based can become a factor in the demise of an organization when faced with significant disruptive competition.

One of the eternal challenges facing any organization is how to handle both innovation and operational excellence properly, since doing so requires a conflict between handling it separately and creating a smooth transition. If there is any organization that can manage to do both well, it will be a very strong organization and one with a very secure base from which to grow further.

That's why, in the field of innovation, we believe long-term, people-focused information should offer a strong sense of what will resonate with individuals in emerging socio-cultural contexts. A company can use information to identify weak signals that help when making decisions about where to focus efforts in business and technology development. And when you conduct your long-term research, you need to be open to anticipating the changing values and mindsets, as well as the behaviours of people and society that will transform future perceptions of value and happiness. (See Chapter 2 for more on this subject.)

WHAT DO YOU NEED TO FOCUS ON?

What follows are a few fundamental points that will help to organize your innovation.

Distinguish between incremental and radical innovation

During our careers, we have used mainly the "1 to 3 horizon model" – described in McKinsey & Company's *The Alchemy of Growth* (Baghai, Coley and White, 2000) – to set a clear scope for innovation activities. You can, of course, use any theoretical framework you like but, whichever you choose, it is vital to distinguish between clearly incremental innovation and radical innovation activities of your company. Although both are innovation activities, each of them requires the installation of different processes, methods and resources in a company.

Consider areas related to innovation

It is also important to realize that innovation is not the only activity you need to consider and it is not one-dimensional; there are a number of other areas also connected to it. The "ten types of innovation" by the Doblin consultancy firm, explains innovations in process, delivery, offering and finance. For your brand and company to successfully innovate, you will need to take a comprehensive approach to *all* aspects of your operation. Only by doing that can you hope to guarantee that your innovative ideas truly break through to your market.

Know where you want to innovate

Working from your brand positioning and brand architecture, you should clarify the area in which you want your brand to innovate, and then communicate that clearly to your organization. As we wrote in Chapter 7, we agree with Ries and Ries (1998) who said that, "In the long term, expanding your brand will diminish your power and weaken your image." Therefore we suggest installing a brand architecture by clustering your range of products into higher-level propositions. By doing this, your brand story will remain strong while also offering you the opportunity to expand your products and services into your chosen market.

We often see examples of sales driven companies that make several variants, exceptions and variations to their portfolio to gain specific short-term business and profits. However in the long term this can erode the strength of a brand. Creating "meaningful" variants is not necessarily a bad thing, but you must not let it take your eye off innovating at the core of your proposition, and off any potential disruptions.

To continuously innovate so that you can grow your company without weakening your brand, one thing you need to do is distinguish between continuous innovation *within an existing* higher-level proposition (domain and/or category level) and innovating *with a new* higher-level proposition. For us, both are radical innovation methods but with obviously different meanings and consequences. The first approach offers you a big advantage when introducing your innovation to market because it can easily associate with your already well-known brand. At the same time, it will also contribute to the further strengthening of your existing brand story, and for that reason we consider it the most effective innovation for a brand.

The second approach is the opposite of the first. If you want to introduce a new domain and/or category – one

with no association with your current brand story – to the
market, then you will need to prepare for a high investment of your resources. Obviously it is up to your brand to
choose between the two approaches, but we highly recommend innovating within an existing high-level proposition
(domain and/or category). Such continuous innovation will
further strengthen your brand story and widen your offer.

Case Study – Design-led innovation: ambient experience

Back in 2004, Philips Design studied the experiences
of everyone involved in conducting an MRI scan. The
team shadowed doctors, nurses, patients, patients'
family members and others before producing an
end-user journey.

Even today, Yasushi can still remember the picture of
an MRI scanning room that emerged from the flows.
Not only was it untidy, but it also contained a cabinet
without a door in which lay several unprotected scissors,
knives and scalpels. While most people undergoing an
MRI scan know a doctor will not cut them during the
procedure, the sight of such a sloppily maintained environment is likely to make them more anxious and
uncomfortable than they already are. Children would
be even more upset.

For even without the presence of such an unprotected cabinet, an MRI scan is an uncomfortable
experience. Patients must lie in a very narrow, dark
tunnel surrounded by noise. If they move at all – and
children, for whom the experience can be highly
unnerving, tend to move a lot – the scan will have to
be repeated from the beginning, which is neither
effective nor efficient for the hospital (in some countries the cost of first scanning is covered by insurance

but additional costs of rescanning are covered by the hospital). In the worst case, a doctor will have to give an upset child a sedative, something that may not necessarily be safe for them.

All their observations led the team to believe that they could propose a better solution, and that this could be done by understanding the situation from the perspectives of everyone involved. Therefore during 2004 and 2005, with the background research completed, the team produced a few scenarios and created experience demonstrators for both internal and external review.

What the team proposed was a "hotel-like" waiting area: a clean, comfortable space where patients could prepare for the scan and their families could accompany them. For children, the team went a step further and created the Kitten Scanner. This was based on findings by psychologists that children would be more comfortable if they understood in advance what was going to happen to them. So the Kitten Scanner was intended as a playful way for a doctor to describe the scanning process. It was a small toy scanner surrounded by rag dolls and fluffy toys. Children were asked to choose a doll or a toy, which the doctor then placed on the scanner bed, at which point a "monitor" beside it displayed an image of the toy's insides. The whole experience was playful, educative *and* relaxing. But this wasn't the only innovation aimed at children.

Before going into the MRI room for a scan, the doctor would ask a child to choose a theme – such as outer space or underwater – images of which were then projected onto the walls and ceiling of the entire scanning room. The research revealed that children would get nervous when a doctor asked them to hold their breath and start to count, so the team created animated themes synchronized to the doctor's actions. For example, if the child had chosen an underwater theme, then when the doctor asked him or her to hold their breath, a dolphin would dive into the water and look for treasure. When the dolphin surfaced, the child could breathe again.

(Note: ambient experience has been one of the successful innovative businesses for Philips Health Care sector. The ambient experience system has now been installed in multiple hospitals world-wide.)

CHALLENGES TO DESIGN-LED INNOVATION

Installing the High Design principles will lead, we believe, to both radical and incremental innovation and will make it an implicit and ongoing activity within the design function. By installing the High Design principles, you will start to innovate with a truly people-focused approach. Several times in our careers we have been involved in the creation of both radical and incremental innovation. And we, working under the High Design principles with highly talented colleagues, have never found it difficult to come up with radical and breakthrough ideas. The real challenges have been in how to position those ideas, how to communicate them and how to bring them to the market by defining the right business model.

Even if you have a number of breakthrough ideas and concepts, if you cannot bring them to the market and make them a successful business for your brand and company to grow, you have not really innovated. At the same time, the current business paradigm is shifting from a company that creates and offers a ready-made value to targeted audiences, to a value constructed by users when both the brand and the users have been engaged. The role of a user has now changed. It is no longer someone who passively receives products – from an established brand that represents their identity – to satisfy their immediate wants. A user is now someone who co-creates – with trusted partners and leading brands – the values that give life to their requirements, creativity and desires.

So how do you bridge the gap between the creation of innovative ideas (and bringing them to market) with the successful business models of the new paradigm?

CO-INNOVATION (AND A SMOKELESS STOVE)

In his book *Open Innovation: The New Imperative For Creating and Profiting From Technology*, Henry Chesbrough (2006) writes that:

> Open innovation is a paradigm that assumes that firms can and should use external ideas as well as internal ideas, and internal and external paths to market, as the firms look to advance their technology.

While we certainly agree with him that a company should move from closed innovation to open innovation, our key reason for suggesting a move to more "openness" is that it leads to more collaboration – because it involves all stakeholders and possible partnerships and alliances. The key to achieving co-innovation is having a shared end goal on the future needs roadmap (see Chapter 15). It is not a preoccupation with a short-term business goal.

When co-innovating, all stakeholders (end-users, partners, experts, etc.) should involve themselves in the entire process, by seamlessly connecting "concept creation" in order to "bring to market" activities for every aspect of innovation. Doblin's *The Ten Types of Innovation* goes into this in some detail, but we can also provide you with a good example of co-innovation from our own experience.

Philips Design launched a programme called Philanthropy by Design as a part of a larger cultural programme. (See

Chapter 15 for more about this.) The Philanthropy by Design
Initiative was launched by Stefano Marzano in 2005, when
Philips Design organized an event entitled "A Sustainable
Design Vision – Design for Sense and Simplicity" in
Eindhoven, the Netherlands. The designers in Philips Design
offered a number of concepts – created by 250 designers – for
humanitarian propositions that addressed social and environmental issues affecting the more fragile parts of our societies. To prepare for this event Yasushi and the team worked
with a number of leading NGOs (non government organizations) to generate insights that would give a clear focus and a
brief for designers to work from. From the concepts that
Philips Design generated for the event the team then chose a
few for further development. One was called Chulha: it was
a smokeless stove for users at the bottom of the social pyramid. And from the time of the event through to its actual
introduction to market, the team continuously collaborated
with such stakeholders as local NGOs, local entrepreneurs,
local universities, experts and potential users.

Throughout the Chulha project, the team managed to
build a strong network and a working relationship with all
stakeholders (including the end-users), and this in turn gave
the team the basis for a co-creation infrastructure. (See
Chapter 3 for more details about such infrastructures.)
Co-creating with end-users reduces the gap between the
concept creation phase and the market introduction phase.
And it also provides you with the basis for continuous innovation since you are continuously generating new insights.

The team's collaboration during the project was based on
a shared goal, vision and long-term roadmap. Now you
might think it was easy for the team to focus on a long-
term goal, vision and roadmap instead of short-term business opportunities since the project was part of Philips's
philanthropic activities. And that is indeed true; on that
project the team was freed from thinking about any short-
term financial success for Philips. However to successfully

bring the concept to market, it was essential to provide short-term business opportunities for local players. Working on Chulha helped the team to realize that the one thing vital for a successful co-innovation approach is that all stakeholders keep their minds focused on the long-term goal, vision and roadmap and share it with each other.

Please do not misunderstand us; we are not saying that co-innovation does not offer any short-term success. We believe that it potentially offers both short-term *and* long-term success: because by collaborating with various stakeholders, the business opportunities that you can achieve (when covering a wider area of innovation) and develop are bigger than those you could develop only by yourself. What we are saying is that your short-term *and* long-term business development should be carried out on the basis of the long-term goal, vision and roadmap you share with all your stakeholders.

And while we do agree that there is a difference in the way your company's philanthropic activities and focused business activities operate, we also strongly believe that your attitude to both should be the same and that that *attitude* is the key for successful co-innovation.

To conclude this section, we would like to share a quote from Stefano Marzano (1992) on taking responsibility for tomorrow, today:

> The future does not just happen. It is created by those who take on the responsibility for it today. If we are to look forward to a period in the future in which we have a stable environment and can pursue sustainable growth, then we must try to restore the balance in both our natural environment and our social and cultural environment ... But first we need to get a clearer picture of the world we want to reach, of routes we could follow to get there – and of where we are today ...

Design plays a key role in the shift towards a sustainable future. Due to its very nature of bridging sociocultural developments and technology, design is a powerful engine for sustainable development. And in their privileged role as interpreters and communicators between people and technology, designers can stimulate new ways to satisfy people's needs. In short, they can generate valuable solutions that are economically, socially and environmentally sustainable.

Stefano Marano, *Past Tense, Future Sense*,
2006

THE NEW ROLE OF A BRAND IN CO-INNOVATION

It is the new role of a brand to take the lead in facilitating the creation of a co-innovation platform. To do this a brand needs to be recognized as a trusted leader – not only by all its stakeholders, but also by the general public. And, in order to achieve this, you first need to find the right partners; partners who can share your vision, goal and long-term roadmap. You then need to earn their trust that you are genuinely aiming for, and highly committed to achieving, that goal more than you are looking for short-term success. Your vision and your goal should come from – and should authentically reflect – your brand values and beliefs. And your company should truly behave according to your brand vision and beliefs.

For us, the most important element of the co-innovation approach is that you possess a clear vision of how to contribute to the short- and long-term happiness and prosperity of people and society. Innovating is like having a conversation: you share your brand vision with, and receive feedback from, both people and society. And together you develop it further.

9

Commitment 9: Give Your Value Proposition the Four Design Drivers

Although he is no longer an active sportsman, one sport Yasushi was passionate about during his student days was skiing. Now that he's stopped, he admits to being completely out of touch with current equipment and trends, but he still remembers a number of well-known brands from that time that he yearned to own. One of them was a pair of ski boots from a classic French brand.

During a recent European winter, quite by accident, he found a shop owned by the brand, and discovered that it had extended its product range beyond ski equipment to position itself as "the mountain sports company". For Yasushi, this had been the brand for true professionals and had produced the best skiers' bindings and boots. But the extended product range erased for him the original brand image: he could no longer tell what made it unique from other mountain sports brands.

Later, when we learned that it had become part of a major sport brand group, we understood the changes that had been made. But for both of us it was a typical example of brand extension that, while no doubt benefitting the company's sales, ruined the authenticity of the original brand.

It reminded us of something Ries and Ries wrote in their *22 Immutable Laws of Branding*: that extending a brand might bring added sales in the short term but in the long term will only diminish its power and weaken its image. It's a statement we fully agree with: your brand image and association is *stronger* if you have *fewer* propositions in your market. So while we believe it is very important for a brand to manage its portfolio carefully, at the same time it is also important to plan a strategic extension of a proposition to maximize the value.

If you agree that "fewer propositions equal a stronger brand", then it is essential for a brand to ensure that its propositions are of maximum value: a business will need fewer of them to fulfil its business value. This is where the four design drivers come in. Each one will, if used properly, help you to refine and maximize the propositions that will offer you the greatest business and brand value.

FOUR DESIGN DRIVERS

The four drivers are:

- Meaningful – experience across the customer journey
- Distinctive – identity to differentiate propositions
- Attractive – and intuitive interaction with surprise and delight
- Coherence – through all touchpoints.

Meaningful

The aim of the *meaningful* driver is to fully explore your chosen proposition so that it offers a full brand experience for your target audiences.

One way to resolve the dilemma between the extension of a product range (leveraging your strong brand) and maintaining a strong brand image is to elevate your value proposition to a higher level instead of placing it on a product level. For example, Dove is a Unilever brand that could place its proposition at the level of the product (i.e. a moisturizing health and beauty soap). Instead, they have chosen to elevate it to the level of "real beauty".

If you do the same, your brand story will not only remain strong, but you will also have the opportunity to expand your product and service offers. We call this "maximizing the value of one proposition". To do this, it's important to create a clear scenario and business roadmap for a proposition that creates a unique experience in the market. Therefore you should use the *meaningful* driver to explore all the opportunities for enriching a chosen proposition (an ownable, unique experience) and expanding (full exploration) it to its full business potential.

Here are some key questions to help you do this:

- Have you fully generated foresights (provision for any future issues that might arise) and insights about your targeted context, and do you have meaningful solutions that fit that context: which users, what activities, which places and over what time scale?

- Have you fully uncovered people's short- and long-term needs?

- Have you explored the full "eco system" (James F. Moore originated the strategic planning concept of a business eco system) and considered all possible products, services and other touchpoints across all domains and categories? (See Chapter 7 for more about domains and categories.)

Figure 9.1 shows a simple two-axis mapping tool you can use to plan the positioning of your proposition against

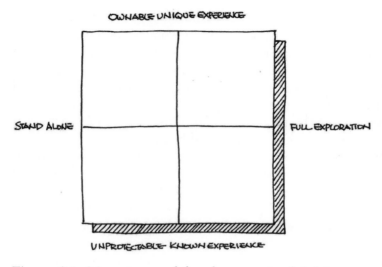

Figure 9.1 *Mapping tool for the meaningful driver*

others in the market. Those that achieve "full exploration" can be considered to offer an "ownable'" unique experience. For example, in the top right corner lies Apple. Apple (and this includes the Apple–Nike collaboration) is one of the best examples of a company maximizing its brand experience and value proposition. Although Apple is acting in only one domain or category with one value proposition, it has managed to grow into one of the biggest companies in the world.

By way of contrast, the bottom left corner of Figure 9.3 shows a standalone product without an actual competitive uniqueness, in this case a kettle or a DVD player from a discount store. In the top left corner are a number of ownable unique products whose product and service offering have yet to be fully explored. They have a unique proposition and a distinctive appearance but remain standalone propositions.

Distinctive

The aim of the *distinctive* driver can be summed up this way: to articulate your proposition by using distinctive benefits with iconic personality.

A category code is something established in the language of a specific product category over a number of years. And if you walk down a supermarket aisle you will see category codes in action: tea and coffee, cereals, beauty products and consumer electronics all have distinct and differentiated categories expressed through certain codes.

A very simple example is toothpaste, for which the packaging is usually full of lots of bright whites, blues, reds and greens, as well as highlights and scientific diagrams of each brand's efficacy. But some brands deliberately break these codes in order to stand out. For example, in Japan, one brand uses black in both its paste and packaging (and also to endorse its "Reason to Believe", which is based on including charcoal in the paste to remove plaque and stains). In some extreme cases this risks a strong rejection by consumers because the product doesn't conform to their perceptions or cultural expectations.

Bottles offer another example. There are definite category code shapes in bottles containing water, cooking oils, liquor and dressings and you actually unconsciously recognize the product on offer through these coded bottle shapes. Quite often, such codes are based on the success of one brand in a category, which then becomes a recognizable code for others to follow. One famous example is a soy sauce bottle designed by GK Design. Its unique shape – designed to fit on a dinner table – has become a symbolic icon for all soy sauce bottles throughout – and outside – Japan.

Therefore to take absolute leadership in your category it is important to come up with a unique proposition (one for which you can claim ownership) that can change the rules of

130 BRAND ROMANCE

the game in that category. Your design group should therefore use the *distinctive* driver to manifest and underpin your unique proposition (ownable benefits) by communicating it with a completely new (iconic) design – which may in turn become a new design for the category it inhabits.

Here are some key questions to help you do this:

- Do you have clear and compelling customer or user insights based on the context?

- Have you defined distinctive, different and ownable benefits, supported by the reasons to believe and the experience?

- Have you articulated these benefits into an original visual language?

- Have you understood and challenged existing category codes to achieve an iconic archetype with unique personality?

Figure 9.2 shows a simple two-axis mapping tool you can use to plan the positioning of your proposition against others in the market, one that offers ownable benefits with an "iconic" design. Dyson, in the top right corner, is one of the best examples of such a proposition. The Dyson brand manifests its unique proposition – the most technologically innovative vacuum cleaner in the world – with an iconic design that, when it was launched, broke the category codes. By way of contrast, the products in the bottom left corner simply follow existing categories – kettle, hair dryer and simple DVD player – and have no specific unique propositions. In the bottom right corner are a number of products with a unique design but no ownable benefits: products that are well designed but easily copied by others.

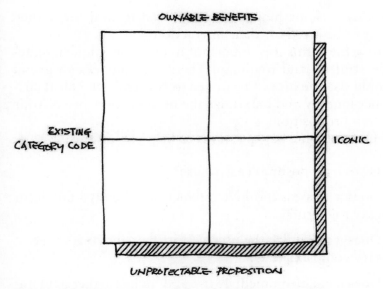

Figure 9.2 *Mapping tool for the distinctive driver*

Attractive

The aim of the *attractive* driver is this: to achieve an intimate engagement with your audiences; to make your proposition attractive and intuitive (easy to learn and hard to use incorrectly); and to provide interaction surprises that delight to create ultimate engagement.

To achieve an intimate, emotional bond with your audiences through your interaction, you need to create not only easy-to-use (intuitive) products, but also pleasurable surprises (engagement). During a television interview a Japanese Michelin star chef in Tokyo used the French word *étonner* ("amaze" in English) to explain the spirit of creation behind surprise experiences in his restaurant, experiences designed to achieve an emotional connection with, and memorable experiences for, his customers. We believe *étonner* is something all brands need to aim for if they want to be loved for their interaction.

To achieve this it is important to create a unique interaction strategy and roadmap. Therefore your design group should use the *attractive* driver to construct the ideal customer journey and maximize the brand experience of your chosen proposition.

Here are some key questions to help you do this:

- Is your proposition easy to use?

- Does it possess intuitive interaction (already known, or easy to learn)?

- Does it minimize the user's effort by removing unnecessary complexity?

- Does it enable immediate use and invite further exploration, offering relevant choices when needed?

- Is it easily recognized, understood and remembered with a minimum of conscious effort?

- Does it engage all relevant senses (for example, with lighting effects, sound quality, scent and tactile interaction), maximizing their pleasure when the product is in use?

- Have you improved its usability from previous propositions?

Figure 9.3 shows a simple two-axis mapping tool you can use to plan the positioning of your proposition against others in the market, one that provides an "intuitive" interaction to achieve an ultimate engagement with your audiences. Again Apple appears in the top right corner because it not only offers intuitive interaction, but also builds in a number of surprising elements designed to create a "tongue-in-cheek" sense of delight. (For example, on a recent visit

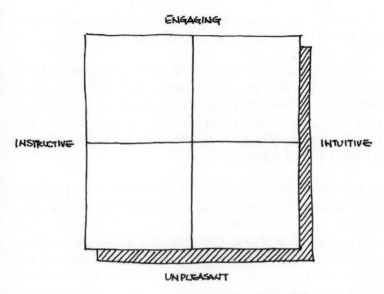

Figure 9.3 *Mapping tool for the attractive driver*

to London we needed to go to an address written down in an email. When one of us accidentally touched the address *in* the email itself, the maps app opened automatically to show us where we were and what route we should take to reach our destination.) By way of contrast, ordinary video and TV remote controls can be placed in the left bottom corner of Figure 9.3.

Coherent

The aim of the *coherent* driver is this: to create one clear, compelling and coherent experience for target audiences, and to deliver it consistently through all possible touch-points in the most effective manner.

In his book *Brand Sense*, Martin Lindstrom touched on the introduction by Singapore Airlines of their "Singapore

girl" in 1973 as an example of breaking through traditional branding barriers. He wrote that:

> the fabric design itself was based on the patterns in the
> cabin décor: Staffers were primped and styled all the
> way down to their makeup. Stewardesses were offered
> only two choices of colour combinations based on a
> specific palette designed to blend in with Singapore
> Airline's brand colour scheme.

To create a seamless brand experience for your proposition, it is important to create a unique (distinctive) and
consistent approach in your touchpoints. Therefore your
design group should use the coherent driver to produce
touchpoints – based on the proposition itself and on the
targeted end-users and customers – that break away from
any conventional approach.

Here are some key questions to help you do this:

- Do you have one clear, consistent and compelling story
  focused on the audience?

- In that story, have you communicated the "reasons to
  believe" and the "experience"?

- Have you explored all possible touchpoints to reach the
  target audience effectively?

- Have you achieved distinctiveness in all touchpoints?

- Have you refined and reduced design elements to focus
  attention on the essentials?

Figure 9.4 shows a simple two-axis mapping tool you can
use to plan the positioning of your proposition against others in the market, one that offers a "distinctive" experience
in your touchpoints to achieve consistency. Singapore
Airlines – as suggested in the introduction to this driver – is

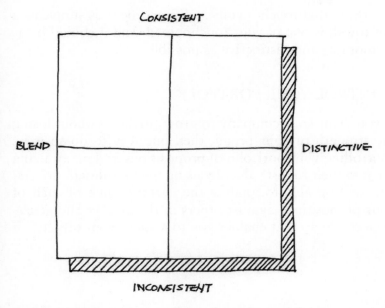

CONSISTENT

BLEND   DISTINCTIVE

INCONSISTENT

Figure 9.4 *Mapping tool for the coherent driver*

a good example for the top right corner of Figure 9.4 since they are one of the pioneers of unique and consistent approaches to touchpoints. In *Brand Sense*, Lindstrom says about them that:

> The sensory branding of the Singapore Girl reached its zenith by the end of the 1990s, when Singapore Airlines introduced Stefan Floridian Waters. Stefan Floridian Waters not only created the fragrance in the flight attendants' perfume, it was blended into the hot towels served before take-off and generally permeated Singapore Airlines' entire fleet. This patented fragrance has since become an unmistakable, distinct trademark of Singapore Airlines.

Anything that touches your audiences, be it as simple as a hot towel, is one of your touchpoints! And it should be as memorable and distinctive as possible.

CONTROL YOUR PORTFOLIO

If you want your company to grow further without losing the strength of your brand, then one way to do so is by controlling your portfolio of propositions and maximizing them to their fullest value. By using the four design drivers, you will be able to analyse the current value of each of your propositions against others in the market and generate a roadmap that enables you to achieve your target.

Part 4

Know How You Will Bring It to Your Audience

10
Commitment 10: Create a Clearly Recognizable Identity

If you need help from security personnel in a public space, it's a good thing that they wear an easily recognizable uniform, isn't it? The same applies to shop assistants. In both cases their uniforms have been created, and applied, to be easily recognized. The uniforms also represent rational, and therefore emotional, values. They function *rationally* because they make the wearer's function and role immediately recognizable. They function *emotionally* because they represent such qualities as authority, trust and safety, both to the people who wear them and to the people who see them.

It's the same for a brand. A brand gains its recognition by the way it uses touchpoints to differentiate itself from other brands. Audi, for example, maintains a very strong identity in all its products and in all the ranges in each product. The Audi brand identity is not only clearly recognizable everywhere, it also offers its audiences the emotional association of quality and trust (its slogan, *Vorsprung durch Technik*, translates as "advantage through technology"), and dignity and pride to its employees.

So how do you create a clearly recognizable identity? That is the question we want to answer in this chapter. And the first aspect we want to touch on is that of brand design identity principles.

BRAND DESIGN IDENTITY PRINCIPLES

In Chapter 7, we pointed out that the brand circle contains a brand design identity principle.

Brand design identity principles are fundamental to a brand and a brand's creative director needs to ensure that they occur throughout the brand. They should express depth of expression across all touchpoints and width of expression to cover the whole brand portfolio. They should describe a high-level approach (my mental model would be Dieter Rams' "ten principles of good design") for your brand's behaviour and appearance. The approach should be one that is firmly based on your brand values and beliefs, and which enables you to orchestrate your brand and create a single brand experience.

Brand design identity principles can be constructed from two components: product and service design, and communication design. For product and service design, the key attributes can consist of appearance, interaction style, material and finish applications, constructions, build quality and so on. For communication design, the key attributes can consist of photographic style (product, life style, etc.), headlines (tone of voice) and colour, environment and so on.

Remember that these principles manifest your brand values and beliefs – they do not describe specific design details. For example, if we mention colour as an aspect of communication design, we are not talking about your selection of pantone colours, but about the qualities of your brand you want particular colours to express (fresh, monochrome, neutral, pure, rich, showy, soft or vivid, for example).

TWO APPROACHES TO A RECOGNIZABLE BRAND

We believe there are two approaches to the creation of a recognizable design identity. The first is "uniformity". The second is "connected diversity". We would like to start by discussing uniformity.

A uniform identity

Although the concept of uniformity may provoke some negative images (strict rules, no freedom) in designers, it remains a highly effective way of visualizing each and every element – products and services – of your proposition in the market. One of the biggest advantages it achieves is immediate recognition. But you can also use it to increase familiarity with your user interface (thereby making recognition easier for your loyal customers) by applying uniform interaction principles. For instance, some auto industry brands apply the same user interface principles throughout their ranges. This means that if you are familiar with one range of car, then driving another car from the same brand won't involve a complicated new learning curve. And there is obviously also a cost advantage to be gained by streamlining the number of parts used by each proposition in a range.

Diversity within uniformity

Such uniformity doesn't however have to exclude diversity. Travelling to and from the Netherlands, we often fly with the Dutch KLM airline and, over the years, have noticed variations in the uniforms of several of the flight attendants. Although each one wears a recognizable KLM jacket, some jackets sport different numbers of silver strips on their sleeves, denoting different grades of seniority. So what the strips do, within a uniform framework, is display the differences between individuals within a group of KLM employees. In the same way, you need to find a way to differentiate the products and services you offer by introducing a system that makes it obvious who their producer is while, at the same time, making clear the differences between the premium and economy ranges.

How do you apply uniformity?

In most cases, when applying the uniform approach, design teams should make very detailed identity guidelines for all products, user interfaces and communications. Creative directors should then install and lead a steering committee to direct, nurture and maintain those guidelines (including the planning for any necessary renewal of the identity) and the team needs to communicate and train all stakeholders to follow them. If necessary, they should install a help desk to provide support. All requests for an exception need to be discussed and agreed by the committee.

You must also construct a clear evaluation and renewal calendar for the future. This is necessary so that you can monitor the validity and effectiveness of your uniform design framework in the market and, when needed, renew your design identity to meet its desired end. We are aware that you may feel odd setting a calendar to renew your identity while you're also creating it, but it is essential that you do this: because if you meet any resistance when introducing a new identity, you will also meet the same amount of resistance when you try to renew it. To avoid this (and keep your organization functioning efficiently) you need to structure, and monitor, the renewal process right from the beginning.

Uniformity in various product types

Although we firmly believe uniformity is a very effective way of applying a strong identity, you may think this will not work if you need to cover several product types. We can think of several examples of a strong uniform identity applied to one type of product: cars. Those produced, for example, by BMW, Audi and Porsche, all share the same elements (lights, radiator grill, windows, etc.). This makes it easier to create different product ranges for a single brand; but if you have various product types, applying one uniform design identity to them all will be a challenge.

Philips applied a very strong and well-organized uniform identity to all the product types in its health care category. This made sense since it wanted to show that many of its health care products "belonged" to each other and worked together. It also wanted to share common parts within the range; this resulted in audience recognition, cost effectiveness and uniform interaction principles, which in turn helped minimize training time and lowered the risk of mistakes during medical treatment.

Connected diversity identity

This is the second approach to creating a recognizable identity for the various product categories of a single brand. Connected diversity identity enables you to achieve a recognizable identity across product categories where there is little similarity in several elements (for example, the headlights and front grille of a car). It enables you to express an identity based on shared values, while at the same time providing you with the opportunity to express the unique value of an individual product. For an example, you need look no further than a family.

When you look at a family over several generations, you notice resemblances among the individuals. Obviously they are not identical, but from a visual point of view they will share common elements through their DNA and they will also (probably) share their family values and beliefs. These manifest themselves in individual behavioural characteristics. It is the same for people from different cultures: individuals might share some common elements through DNA (such as dark hair among Asians) but they will also – usually – share the cultural values of their background, which then manifest themselves as individual behavioural characteristics. (I'm sure we've all heard someone say, "That's a typical American", at some point, or "How British".)

However although connected diversity identity works just like a family or cultural identity, it is based more on shared "(cultural) values" and communicates these more through behavioural characteristics than purely visual elements. It's an approach that requires the design team to immerse itself in, and share the values of, a proposition so that it can then orchestrate its articulation across the required range of products. (See Chapter 15 on creating a shared culture for more about applying a cultural programme to do this.)

When using the connected diversity identity approach, the creative director (and/or brand creative director – see Chapter 1) becomes a missionary who helps the team (by continuously reminding) to understand the values. It is this shared understanding, much more than the use of written guidelines, that helps orchestrate the articulation of values across a product range. That said, it is also possible to apply a number of tools (visualization by images, for example) to share an understanding of the values with the team.

We are strong believers in the connected diversity identity approach, which is in turn based on brand design architecture (see Chapter 7). That's why, in your brand layer, your identity should not only consist of such brand assets as the company logo, name and colour, but should also specify brand behavioural characteristics that reflect the brand's values, beliefs and personality. Based on the brand layer's behavioural characteristics, you can apply either another level of connected diversity identity or uniform identity to the domain and/or category circle.

Case Study – Philips–Alessi

The Philips–Alessi range is a good example of the connected diversity identity. In 1994, Philips and Alessi introduced a range of kitchen appliances with the co-branded name Philips–Alessi under the leadership of Stefano Marzano. The four products in the range were presented as a family, but a family of four individuals with certain resemblances rather than a uniform identity. The family relationship was reflected in the common way they projected abstract qualities through such "elements" as form language, materials, colour and user interface design. The stability that resulted from the sturdy shape and large footprint, for instance, increased the feeling of the product's reliability. As a result, the Philips–Alessi products each possessed a different character, while still fitting into a family (value proposition) identity.

The family identity consisted of such elements as:

- Rounded, sturdy forms to give the message of reliability, durability and stability as well as friendliness, affection and warmth

- New materials with extra thickness to give the right warm quality and a pleasant sound when tapped

- Simplified functions that were easy and pleasant to use

- Colours expressing warmth, individuality and timelessness

- Elements such as a chrome spout to express professional quality and provide a link to other Alessi products. These also provided an identity signature element running throughout the range.

DO YOU MAKE A BRAND SIGNATURE PART OF A BRAND IDENTITY?

As a part of brand identity, we would like also to touch on the creation of a recognizable element, the so-called "signature" of your brand.

The *Oxford English Dictionary* defines a signature as:

- A person's name written in a distinctive way as a form of identification in authorizing a cheque or document or concluding a letter

- The action of signing a document: *the licence was sent to the customer for signature*

- A distinctive pattern, product, or characteristic by which someone or something can be identified: *the chef produced the pâté that was his signature* [Or, as modifier]: *his signature dish.*

Most of the companies (with the exception of Muji) that we are aware of in the market use their brand name (and/or logo, if it is available) to 1) denote their products and services, and 2) to communicate and encourage the recognition of their brand – literally, placing a signature under their brand promise. But a key question remains: do you need something more than your brand name and logo as the recognizable signature for your identity?

From the point of view of identity, any element will become a signature as long as people recognize it as the unique icon of its brand. Or, to put it another way, if people do not recognize the element as your signature – even though you may think it is – then it is not your brand's real signature.

The most common approach to applying a signature can be found in the automobile industry, where it is standard practice to add the signature elements to the headlights and front grille of the car, and not just because these are usually the most visible parts of the vehicle; they are also made to perform a function, so that they do not become merely decorative. (BMW's front grille – the kidney grille – is a well-known signature of its automobiles.)

It is also important to remember that the signature does not always need to be a visual element: it can work on the other senses. (The sound a closing BMW car door makes is a good example.)

WHY CREATE AN IDENTITY?

In this chapter we have touched on two approaches to the creation of an identity and the application of a signature. The rational purpose of either of these approaches is the same: create recognition to differentiate. By creating instant recognition you give your audiences easy access to your brand values and beliefs, because people make emotional associations when you display a unique, distinctive and recognizable identity. Your targeted audiences may associate it with quality, which will in turn make them trust your brand. Such an identity may also affect your internal stakeholders, creating pride in them that they belong to your brand. And if it does, then that pride will increase the hope and stamina they require to reach the next goal of your brand.

This means that whatever approach you take to your identity it must be an authentic expression of your brand values and beliefs, as well as one that is meaningful and relevant to your audiences. Anything that is not based on your brand, expressing your values and beliefs – or that is not meaningful and relevant to your audiences – is merely decoration.

11

Commitment 11: Embrace the Three Design Principles

Do you remember being disappointed as a child when you received the wrong present at Christmas? During the writing of this book, we discovered that when we were children, and still believed in Santa Claus, Yasushi used to write him a postcard letting him know what presents he wanted. It was his mother's suggestion and he still remembers walking to the post box with her every December to post the card. One year, he asked for a toy robot; and not just any robot but a specific kind. But the robot that arrived on Christmas morning wasn't the robot he had asked for. Knowing the role his mother had played in learning what was wanted (writing a postcard was her way of finding out) and the role his father had played in buying the present, it was obvious that there had been a failure in the system that year.

Is this a situation you recognize? When you need to prepare for some special occasion – such as buying a birthday present for your loved ones – what approach do you use? We assume that your first step is to find out what they want (in business terms: building your insights). Or perhaps you might say that finding out isn't needed: that you already know what they want because you keep up to date with their wishes on a daily basis (in business terms: continuously building your insights).

Then, knowing what they want (if you're lucky, they have only one thing in mind), what do you do? The second step, we would imagine, is to evaluate the list and choose the one (or more) gift you want to give. Then comes the simple (though sometimes not always so simple) third step of finding and buying it.

Without knowing it, what you are actually doing when making such plans is – unconsciously – applying three design stages. The three steps involved in buying a present match the three stages at the core of a design process – the three stages required to fulfil the principles of High Design:

- Understanding and exploration
- Proposition and direction setting
- 360° experience creation.

You should of course always construct a process that best fits your organization and culture. But these three stages are, for us, the key to good design and are applicable to almost everyone.

UNDERSTANDING AND EXPLORATION

To fulfil a "people-focused" approach in your design work, you should always make sure you have all the necessary information about people's foresights (provision for future issues) and insights. (See Chapter 2 for more on short- and long-term needs.) Working from these, your design team can then explore several scenarios to find the most valuable proposition for your target market. You should focus on:

- Identifying long-term needs
- Producing innovative, next-generation products and services by responding to today's problems and un-met needs

- Exploring innovative new solutions as hypothetical scenarios to fulfil short- and long-term needs.

As you work, don't forget to ask yourself the following questions, to challenge both yourself *and* the company:

- How well do you know your customers and users?

- How can you genuinely be outside-in? What more can you do?

- Can you fulfil your customers' needs even before they're aware of that need?

- How well do you know yourself? (What is your vision/mission?) Remember: you must know yourself before you can act effectively.

- Have you fully uncovered people's desires, values and needs (both rational and emotional) throughout their entire experience?

As you work, you may encounter some pitfalls. Some of the most common are that you:

- End up designing for yourself, not for your customers and users

- Skip this stage too easily

- Use research to try to prove what *you* want or believe

- Accept weak, shallow or superficial insights

- Fail to see understanding your customers' or users' needs as an ongoing activity.

PROPOSITION AND DIRECTION SETTING

You need to evaluate and then select your final proposition for your market based on the scenarios you have explored (which are underpinned by your foresights and insights). It is extremely important that your propositions always reflect your brand values and beliefs, and that they also articulate the essence of those values and beliefs concisely. You should focus on:

- Maximizing the proposition for business and brand value
- Establishing the essence of the proposition and ensuring that it is appropriately translated for all stakeholders.

As you work, don't forget to ask yourself the following questions:

- How accurately can you articulate/capture your proposition (in its essence)?
- Does it genuinely reflect customer insights and genuinely manifest your brand promise?
- Have you explored the full "eco system" and considered all possible products, services and other touchpoints across all categories?

Be careful to avoid the following common pitfalls:

- Your articulation is too long and too vague
- You accept stereotypes in place of real insights
- You do not fully explore the opportunity and fail to "iterate" enough
- You skip this stage and go straight to the next.

360° EXPERIENCE CREATION

Based on the chosen design direction for your proposition, make sure you have properly articulated it for all touchpoints.

It is very important that every team member be fully immersed in the essence of your brand and proposition, so that you do not lose sight of a truly outside-in (people-focused) proposal. As you work through this stage, you should ensure that you:

- Create a full brand experience, ensuring that each touch point contributes to the articulation of the proposition at every point on a customer's journey.

As you work, don't forget to ask yourself the following questions:

- How can you create a fully authentic and ongoing customer experience?

- Have you fully explored all relevant touchpoints and used them in an intelligent manner?

- Have you been as consistent as possible throughout all the touchpoints (including the way your customer-facing staff behaves)?

Be careful to avoid the following common pitfalls:

- You make subjective aesthetic choices; you think of design as "styling"

- You don't think from the outside-in

- You don't consider how best to reach your audience *or* you only use known touchpoints

- You take only this step and not the others

- You have too little time and/or money

- You treat it as a factory

- You deal with touchpoints separately throughout the process, and so risk them being inconsistent (as well as failing to build up sufficient experience)

- You think you have to create the entire eco-system yourself. (You may well need to work with other companies to do so.)

TOO MANY STAGES?

If you're a designer, you've probably been asked by a client at one time or another: "Can you start designing (usually meaning, produce sketches) immediately?" For some reason, many people involved in their own business forget the principles we nearly all take when setting out to buy a present for a loved one. They skip stages one and two – research and evaluation – because they think it will be faster and cheaper to go straight to stage three: finding the actual present. But is it? Can you imagine yourself running into a shop to buy a present for someone without knowing what they really want? Is it not fair to say that if you take the time to fully understand their wishes in advance, you will save yourself time in the final phase – and come up with a better result?

This is why we believe that by applying *all three* of these stages your design work will become *more* efficient and effective. Your work during *understanding and exploration* helps the quality and speed of the *proposition and direction-setting* stage, which in turn has the same effect on *360° experience creation*. It's our firm belief that you can enable full effectiveness by applying all three stages to your design process. You can also use each step in each stage as your quality assurance system.

Furthermore, we would also suggest that you treat each stage as parallel, rather than linear, actions. By doing this, you will make it possible to take quick action should you need to. To return to the analogy of buying a present, by being with your loved ones on a daily basis, you will prob-

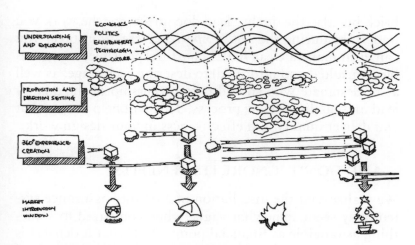

Figure 11.1 *The three design stages*

ably already have a good idea of what they want – instead of having to take the time to find out. That's why we would suggest running the first stage – *understanding and exploration* – as part of your annual programme: it will ensure that you always have necessary access to the predictions and insights you require to take another step. Figure 11.1 illustrates all three stages in operation.

INTRODUCE A QUALITY ASSURANCE SYSTEM...

If you do manage to create your process with clear deliverables based on the three design stages, you should also then install a quality assurance system by introducing quality lead and quality review.

In principle, the deliverables of one stage are the quality lead for the next stage. For example, if you have clear deliverables at the end of *proposition and direction setting* – such as a "proposition document" and/or a "design direction-setting document" – they will become not only a brief, but also the quality lead documents for the work you undertake during the *360° experience creation* stage. You can even make a clear RACI chart (responsible, accountable, consulted and informed) to describe each stage, as well as to designate who should take ownership of the quality lead and quality review process. This will help ensure that you deliver quality and effectiveness in your design work.

...AND DON'T IGNORE ITS BENEFITS

We realize that the installation of a quality assurance system may seem somewhat vague when compared to something as tangible as financial points. But what it delivers is the chance to make a very clearly structured system of accountability.

Not only that, but you'll find – when you review the quality of the work produced – that you can also use the opportunity to discover newly developed content, process, methods and tools, which you can then share throughout your organization. Furthermore it's also a good time for your senior managers to review and identify any missing capabilities that may need further development. (For more on both these points, see Chapter 15.)

CUSTOMIZE!

To make the most of your design thinking and business capability, you should integrate the design process fully into your company's business creation process. Start by finding the design process that best suits your purpose, then use the three stages described in this chapter as its basis. And when making your process description for each of the three stages, it's also useful to make a data bank of your tools, methodology and best cases. For this, it would be ideal if your company could support you with an IT tool that would enable your design community to share all their best case studies throughout the entire organization.

FULFIL EACH STAGE!

It is up to your organization to decide how much detail is needed to describe your design process. It is also up to your organization to decide how much time you would like to spend on each phase. These are your decisions to make. However if you really love your audiences, then you must fulfil each step of each of the three stages we've described here. For this, there is no short cut.

12
Commitment 12: Create One Vocabulary for the Whole Organization

Once you have clearly integrated the design process into your company's business creation process, the next challenge you face will be to create a shared vocabulary for all the functions outside the design disciplines (such as business strategies, marketing and engineering). Such a vocabulary will enable your company to get the best out of its own resources and networks.

Back in the 1990s, Yasushi once came across a series of cartoon-like sketches, beautifully drawn by a colleague who had previously worked for a car manufacturer. The story the cartoons told was very simple. It started with an image of a meeting packed with participants from various functions – engineering, marketing, design and so on – who were all given the same brief: to develop a car. The sketches then showed the different cars dreamed up by each function.

It's unfortunate that copies no longer exist to be shared here, because misunderstanding and miscommunication are the classic ingredients for comedy, and the sketches showed – very amusingly – how easily people can misunderstand each other, even when they all speak the same language. (Something that is actually due to the limitation of using just words to describe a plan – especially using adjectives to describe an emotional aspect. Verbal communication is always open to the wrong interpretation by a listener.) However Neil has found a similar example in the book *Total Quality Management* by J. Oakland (1989). It's uncertain who originally drew the cartoon, but it comes as close to the car design sketches as anything we've seen. The cartoon shows different swings, the first as the marketing department requested it, and then each department's different interpretation of a swing with increasing levels of complexity and finally a sketch of what the customer actually wanted, which was a simple tyre hung from a rope from a tree.

It also illustrates why we believe Design can play an integrator's role: because it can use all its skills to translate topics into tangible forms based on an understanding of cultural meanings throughout the business creation process. It can offer one vocabulary for all the functions. In this chapter we would like to share some approaches that may help you to create such a vocabulary.

CREATE A MOOD BOARD

Although it is a standard, well-known approach, a mood board remains a very useful aid when creating a shared vocabulary for the design team, and we're sure many design professionals still use one to help visualize possible direction settings, target audiences, competitive fields and so on. The number can vary, from a single inspirational board to multiple boards for different aspects of a project.

It is also good practice to consider the type of images you use and to ensure that you pick words that capture the key qualities of an experience. Images can range from abstract – capturing an emotion – to literal examples of objects. Combining words with images can help clarify the mood you want to create.

VISUALIZE YOUR TARGET AUDIENCES BASED ON AN UNDERSTANDING OF CULTURAL VALUES

When you possess the data you need to create personas of your target audiences, you can then visualize the life of those personas by showing not only images of them, but also of the environments they may occupy: houses, working environments, places they visit. A persona is a fictional creation, but once you have the data generated by your co-creation activities (See Chapter 3 for more about co-creation) it will be easy to apply all the photos of such "real" environments. Personas really do help an organization focus on customers and users, and not just a stereotype of a segment but a real person with real values and needs. They can help a team look at the product, service or brand, etc. through the eyes of that person.

VISUALIZE YOUR END-USERS AND THE CUSTOMER JOURNEY BASED ON AN UNDERSTANDING OF CULTURAL VALUES

Creating visual maps of real or possible customer journeys is an excellent tool not only for visualizing and sharing certain processes people go through – and the contexts in which they go through them – but also for use in brainstorming sessions. You can discuss, capture and identify unmet needs, as well as brainstorm potential solutions within cross-functional teams. Ask your participants to bring real pictures of the environments and situations encountered at specific customer journey points to enrich your sessions.

As discussed in Chapter 2, the timeframe of this customer journey can be adjusted to support different types of activity; that is, focussing on the details of buying, installing and using a product can offer the team common challenges and yield excellent opportunities for incremental innovation. Broadening the focus to a specific period, (for example, getting pregnant, through to having young children) can offer opportunities for new propositions and more radical innovation.

CREATE STORYBOARDS

Before you start to set an identity direction, it is important to create a number of storyboards. These are similar to film storyboards, and are very effective for exploring various value proposition scenarios. They can help you set the direction for how you want your audience to experience each value proposition.

CREATE EXPERIENCE DEMONSTRATORS

The storyboards you create can be transformed into images, animations or even simple "experience demonstrators". An experience demonstrator is an extremely effective way of articulating the storyboards of your brand and value proposition experience. It can work at the level of a "laboratory try out" (a somewhat "quick and dirty" internal test of a concept) right up to a more complete, and detailed, manifestation of your experience concepts.

Note that we purposely do not use the word "prototype" here, which, according to the *Concise Oxford English Dictionary*, is defined as a: "trial model or preliminary version of a vehicle, machine, etc."

We use the term "experience demonstrator" instead of prototype because the focus of an experience demonstrator is not to test a fully engineered, or fully serviced, model. You can make an experience demonstrator for one function with completely "fake" technology because it is intended only to test (by imitating a real experience) the specific benefits and functions of a concept. What's important is the experience it delivers.

The sauna

To describe the benefits of creating experience demonstrators, Yasushi quite often uses a story told by Bertrand Rigot (a former colleague and an extremely creative designer) about the sauna to describe the value and power of experience demonstrators.

The sauna is popular all over the world – not just in Scandinavian countries. However imagine for a moment that it doesn't exist, but that you have come up with the idea for it and can only describe it in words. You might start by saying that "It's a small room, very hot and humid inside, where people sit naked". At which point you would probably be asked, "To do what?'", to which you would reply, "To sweat!". We wonder how many people would reply, "What a fantastic idea! I'll put all my company resources into realizing this concept". Not many, we think; the words describe the experience the sauna offers insufficiently.

But by using an experience demonstrator, you could present a far more engaging picture of the sauna's capabilities. The demonstrator would not tell you whether it would be a financial success, or whether it was a concept you should continue developing, but it would at least help you make a judgement based on your gut feeling.

Case Study – The Simplicity Event

We can also offer one practical example of experience demonstrators from our own experience. One of the most challenging, but also rewarding, projects Yasushi worked on in his time at Philips called for the creation of a great many experience demonstrators. It was called The Simplicity Event and it consisted of a series of groundbreaking events intended to 1) reinforce the notion that Philips was a reference point for the concept of "simplicity", and 2) to showcase – and bring to life – the company's innovations. The project comprised three activities: concept creation, experience demonstrator creation and event creation. Between 2005 and 2008, the project team created a series of unique concepts under an annual theme and showcased them two times a year in such locations such as Paris, London, New York, Hong Kong and Sao Paulo.

Yasushi was lucky enough to lead this project and worked intensively with a highly talented team of people to make the series of events a success. To showcase the story in the event, the team chose to manifest each concept scenario as an experience demonstrator. It was highly challenging since the deadline (the opening day of the event) had been set in advance, the invitations had already been sent and there was no chance of postponement. Not only that, but the event was also both a major financial investment for the company and a presentation for the key stakeholders. In other words, the team not only had to finish everything on time but also needed to be successful! You can imagine the pressure on them to deliver working experience demonstrators for all the concepts.

However if you view the results, we believe you can see the rewards that resulted from working under such high pressure. The project was very effective in communicating the concepts – and the company's "simplicity" scenario – because the experience demonstrators it used communicated with the visitors' gut feelings. They didn't need to try to understand the concept "rationally" – by interpreting words – but could react "emotionally" to an actual physical object.

The following links offer some examples of the demonstrators that were used:

> http://www.youtube.com/watch?v=4lRlp61jMpY
> http://www.youtube.com/watch?v=R-Cz144-qyQ
> &feature=related
> http://www.youtube.com/watch?v=TTHtMqHyU
> 4w&feature=related
> http://www.youtube.com/watch?v=6ZfIgdIgXDk
> &feature=related
> http://www.youtube.com/watch?v=-adiqR9b-
> 4o&feature=related

This link – http://vimeo.com/8118794 – will take you to a "making of" video for the 2007 project. When you watch it, you will be able to see what we mean by "laboratory try-outs", since several quick and dirty tests were made before producing the final experience demonstrators.

USE THE PROPOSITION FRAMEWORK

No doubt each of you has a framework you use to capture a value proposition by describing the different marketing elements that define the positioning of a new product in the market – from the standpoint of the end-user. But when you have done that there is one tool that can be used to capture the core essence of a proposition in three basic elements – *the significance*; *the experience* and *the reason to believe* – using the minimum number of words and images. It's called the proposition framework. Although it can be a tough challenge for the cross-functional project team to try to distil concept descriptions into the bare minimum of words and images, this tool will help them to understand

and confirm the core of their proposition. It works effectively for two reasons:

> One: by extracting the essence of value propositions, it helps confirm the essence of the concept you cannot afford to lose because of possible internal compromises. It helps you consciously make your decisions throughout the process by securing the outside-in concept.
> Two: it triggers and guides your creativity, provides clarity in briefings to all creative functions, and ensures a consistent experience of the proposition across all touchpoints.

The significance (my motivation)

Why is this important to me?

The experience (my emotional perception)

How does it make me feel?

The reason to believe (my rational perception)

What is it? What will it do (rationally) for me?

Sinek's golden circle

When Yasushi discovered a speech by Simon Sinek on the TED organization's website – www.ted.com – titled "How Great Leaders Inspire Action", it made him realize that what we do with the proposition framework is very close to Sinek's theory of The Golden Circle. In his book *Start with Why*, Sinek wrote that, "Companies try to sell us *what* they do, but we buy *why* they do it." We agree with him, but we should stress that the core of our message is *the significance* (outlined already), and that it should always reflect your brand values and beliefs.

Sinek (2009) uses Apple as an example of his golden circle theory and describes the core of the company's appeal in the following words:

> Everything we [Apple] do, we believe in challenging the status quo. We believe in thinking differently. The way we challenge the status quo is by making our products beautifully designed, simple to use and user-friendly. And we happen to make great computers. Wanna buy one?

For Sinek the significance of Apple is their credo that they believe in thinking differently; that they offer the experience of "beautiful objects and interfaces"; and that the reason to believe in the company is demonstrated by the Apple products themselves.

As Sinek uses Apple, we quite often use Dyson as an example when describing how people can apply the proposition framework. *The significance* of Dyson is that it offers the most technologically innovative vacuum cleaner in the world. *The experience* of Dyson is the highest vacuuming power: you can vacuum up anything. *The reason to believe* in Dyson is its cyclone technology.

We should add that if this is their proposition framework, then their product design is the perfect answer to their story. For us, Dyson's product design – from a marketing point of view, the way in which it tells its story – is perfect. It shows *the reason to believe* – cyclone technology – by using a transparent cover, and then manifests *the experience* – the highest vacuuming power – with jet engine detail. Dyson changed the whole category of vacuum cleaner by using a unique, iconic design to articulate *the significance* of its product – the most technologically innovative vacuum cleaner in the world – and in so doing completely differentiates its product from other manufacturers. (We touch on iconic design in Chapter 9.)

TRUE COLLABORATION

This chapter has shown examples of how design can use its tools and skills to translate topics into tangible forms based on deep understanding of cultural meanings during the stages of the business creation process, and play an integrator's role by creating one vocabulary. It is design's unique skill to be able to articulate and translate intangible foresights, insights and ideas into something tangible and "discussable" to all stakeholders. It is a fundamental enabler for achieving true collaboration with all stakeholders (both inside and outside).

13

Commitment 13: Recognize the Maestro and the Virtuoso

Although Yasushi is by no means what you might call a classical music fan, he has lived in two countries that are home to two top quality concert halls: Austria and The Netherlands. And because of this he has, on a few occasions, enjoyed performances by some of the best symphony orchestras in the world. When attending such concerts, he has always been amazed by how the musicians manage to perform in such an "orchestrated" manner.

As with any organization, we assume that in addition to the standard day-to-day running of an orchestra, two types of people – carrying out two roles – are also required if it is to perform before an audience. The first sets a direction for the others (conducts them) who then perform (by playing music) their specific roles. Both need to be fully trained and to specialize in what they do, which implies that they are actually carrying out a profession rather than playing a role. We call the first the maestro and the second the virtuoso.

SEAMLESS COLLABORATION

Being the conductor of an orchestra is a profession in and of itself, as is being a musician in an orchestra. And we believe this applies not just to musical environments. For example, in a restaurant, particularly a restaurant in a hotel that often organizes large events, the head chef is a conductor while the various specialist chefs who prepare the dishes such as soup, starter, main course and dessert are the musicians. The head chef has been trained in, and has experience of, conducting such an event – he is the maestro – while a specialist chef such as a *chocolatier* preparing a beautiful chocolate dessert to conclude the event is the virtuoso.

In any profession, when you are trying to conduct a well-orchestrated experience for people, you will face the same challenges as any conductor, musician or chef. And you will therefore need your maestro and virtuoso to collaborate seamlessly and perform their chosen functions as well as they can. If you have ever seen the film of the legendary restaurant *El Bulli*, you may remember the scene in which the head waiter described the process of serving by saying that, "people eat three hours maximum and in their three hours they eat 35 dishes. That's the rhythm." It is remarkable to see how much this restaurant has been "orchestrated" so that all its "players" – the virtuosi – can offer a single, seamless experience for the diners.

We believe that conducting one brand experience through all touchpoints is fundamentally the same as conducting a symphony or a dinner experience. Which is why we also believe its success depends on both a maestro and a virtuoso. A few years ago we worked together with other colleagues in Philips Design on defining these roles, and in this chapter we give a summary of the results of our work.

THE MAESTRO

The maestro's main role is to orchestrate all the touchpoints by leading the design process from start to end. He or she will *conduct* the process. Depending on your brand design architecture (see Chapter 7) and the size of your portfolio, he or she should be dedicated to certain layers (Brand, Domain and/or Category) of your brand design architecture.

For example, if your brand is in the domain and/or category of food preparation, you should dedicate one maestro to it and expect him or her to have a thorough knowledge of, and insights into, food preparation. Both knowledge and insights would be focused on such specific contexts as:

- Location (for example, the kitchen, dining room or garden)

- People (for example, a busy parent with small children or a young couple)

- Time (for example, a busy weekday or a relaxed weekend).

If your brand covers wide portfolios with multiple domains and multiple categories under each domain, you should install a hierarchical maestro structure: one that moves from brand-dedicated maestro through domain-dedicated maestro to category-dedicated maestro.

The maestro's main role

Based on a deep understanding of a focused brand design architecture layer, the maestro's main role is to orchestrate the design strategy and desired brand experience, for each brand and/or value proposition, through all relevant touchpoints. The maestro must be able to orchestrate activities across a broad range of related design disciplines (communication, product, interaction, people research, etc.) to ensure coordinated propositions that will result in a single multi-touchpoint brand experience design programme for the dedicated cluster. (See Chapter 8 for more on this.)

Above all, the most important factor a maestro must possess is a passion for his or her subject. We believe that a maestro sits at the very core of building love with an audience, which means that he or she must be someone whose heart pounds and whose adrenaline races when thinking about their focused cluster. Maestros should want to know everything there is to know about their customers or users and about their activities and needs in this cluster. This focus and passion, coupled with awareness of foresights and insights, should lead to a clear vision of the direction of, and opportunities available to, a focused brand design architecture layer.

The maestro's responsibilities

The maestro will be responsible for:

- Understanding what design does and doesn't know about the focused brand *design* architecture layer

- Understanding the customer's or user's needs

- Developing a roadmap for filling in any missing knowledge – what we call "programming".

The maestro will have – or will develop – a deep knowledge of the dedicated brand design architecture layer (brand, domain and/or category) and an insight into the trends influencing the business. He or she will do this by focusing on it for the longer term and building long-term relationships within it. He or she will have a broad knowledge and understanding of different design and design-related disciplines. (Such a person is sometimes referred to as a "T-shaped" person.)

The maestro's network

The maestro's network is mostly internally focused (within the organization) and works on building long-term relationships with other business stakeholders (although it may also build relevant external networks for the focused, cluster knowledge building). The maestro should be recognized as a key strategic partner – and expert – who is instrumental in generating business value with the company's internal business stakeholders.

The maestro's key tasks

- Lead and orchestrate a clear design strategy and road-map for the focused brand design architecture layer (brand, domain and/or category)

- Lead and orchestrate all design disciplines to create co-ordinated design-led product or service and communication propositions and brand design architecture

- Lead and orchestrate the creation of the relevant brand experience for the focused brand design architecture layer – for each brand and/or value proposition – through all relevant touchpoints.

The maestro's "enabling" tasks

- Manage the career paths of – and coach – the team, developing the capabilities required by the focused brand design architecture layer

- Identify and generate the knowledge required for the focused brand design architecture layer based activity

- Build relationships and develop and share in-depth knowledge of the focused brand design architecture layer.

THE VIRTUOSO

The virtuoso possesses a unique expertise in, and a keen focus on, his or her specific area, not to mention a broad knowledge of, and insight into, a range of different areas of business. Working from Stefano Marzano's philosophy of High Design, you should try to expand your virtuoso expertise outside conventional design capability (by building internal resources or creating external networks) and into such "human science" areas as sociology, psychology, anthropology and cultural ethnology.

The virtuoso's choice

As far as we know, every designer is educated and trained as a virtuoso in a specific field; for example, interaction design, product design, graphic design. We know of no school that offers an educational programme in becoming a maestro (which we touch on in Chapter 14). By default, due to the currently available educational programmes, every designer starts their career as a budding virtuoso. But at certain moments in those careers, each designer needs to choose whether to remain a virtuoso or to develop as a maestro. (We will touch on this further in the Double career path section.) Those who decide to remain a virtuoso will need to increase their expertise and be recognized as a top-level talent in a specific design competence (such as product design, interaction design or communication design). They will also need to gain high external recognition through media exposure by winning awards, becoming an IP (intellectual property) holder and/or the author of published white papers, reports or books.

The virtuoso's focus

The typical focus for a top level virtuoso is a high profile project (for example, mission critical projects, emerging markets, innovation topics of your brand and company) that requires detailed knowledge and strong leadership in a functional competence. The results would usually be internationally recognized as "new" or "advanced" in their field, influence long-term business directions and support innovation.

Top level virtuosos should take the lead in inspiring respected capability communities and platforms. They should lead the development of the competency to anticipate and support the long-term needs of the business. They should also actively develop the team competency profile by networking with international platforms.

The virtuoso's network

The virtuoso's key networking focus should be on external networks for their specialties. This would help build his or her team's competence by ensuring up-to-the-minute knowledge, access to key capabilities and talent, and the maintenance of a profile in that competence.

The virtuoso's key tasks

- Lead and inspire the organization with intellectual leadership and by challenging the paradigm of the competence

- Support innovation by finding the best way to apply his or her competence to projects in the business.

The virtuoso's "enabling" tasks

- Take the lead in building competence, and ensure that the right capability and knowledge is built for the brand and adds value to the business

- Lead the whole competency group, or just one specific area

- Provide first-line expert professional guidance to colleagues and the wider creative community to inspire new design thinking
- Build an internal and external profile – and thought leadership – for the competence
- Develop individuals and teams by investing in the coaching of talent and the development of relevant career paths.

ROLE DESCRIPTIONS FOR MAESTRO AND VIRTUOSO

It is very important to describe clearly the role of each maestro and virtuoso at every seniority level for every function (for example, internal grading discussions, performance reviews, career discussions, annual performance target settings and external job descriptions). One way to construct a role description is to base it on key responsibility, knowhow and influence.

Key responsibility

This describes the required capabilities and skills for specific roles. While creating descriptions of the key responsibilities for about 20 different competencies, we have discovered that you can usually cluster them into three to four core competences.

Knowhow

This describes the required educational level, experience and capability and knowledge.

Influence

This describes the significance of the role: for example, size of budget/turnover; size of business the individual works for; complexity (size, location, etc.) of the team; level of influence and interaction (seniority level) the individual has in the role.

VIRTUOSO: REPLACING TAXONOMY WITH TAGGING

In a design team Yasushi was once part of, one of its members told him she needed a new title because she was starting to expand her expertise into a new field. Although the issue of titles is not one we want to discuss here, we would like to finish this chapter by touching on the subject of a "capability list" and how to recognize people's capabilities by "tagging" them.

In the design industry, unfortunately, we use the same words for design *services* as we do for design *capabilities*. For example, a number of design agencies offer a "product design service". And, as you know, there is a design school course called "product design", which produces graduates called "product designers". So, in this case, does a "product design service" equal "product design capability"? We think this is why we sometimes mix up capability and service.

A product design capability is only one of the capabilities (which obviously plays a major role) that you need to provide a good product design service. To offer a good product design service, following the three core activities (insights and exploration; proposition and direction setting; and experience creation) multiple experts and capabilities will be involved.

When Yasushi joined the design team mentioned here, he was astonished to hear the team members say they could offer over 50 different services. However he soon learned that the differences between those services were actually differences in approaches, methodologies or separate/combined offers. And the reason why one member came to ask for a new title was because she had begun to be involved in a new cluster of services. For us, this is a typically bad example of both service clusters and the mixing of service and capability names.

To solve this problem, we think you first need to clearly separate a virtuoso's capabilities from the list of services offered. We would also suggest that you make such a list from the point of view of what you deliver to your stakeholders instead of how you approach a project (the processes, methods and tools you use).

You then need to install an infrastructure that enables you to clearly recognize a virtuoso's capabilities; not only so you can create a career path for them (which calls for a judgement of their performance) but also so you can provide easy access to the appropriate capabilities of each design phase. To do this you need to have 1) a clear list of all your virtuoso's capabilities, and 2) the chance not to classify but to tag people.

Obviously, you will have a number of people in your team with more than one capability: and we also realize that some people would like a new title to recognize their multiple capabilities. But it will make life for the organization extremely difficult if you start giving each combination a unique name. (In Philips Design, there were over twenty virtuoso capabilities. If we had made combinations of only two of all the capabilities on offer we would have had over 400 titles to remember). So we would suggest the following: to resolve both the employer and employee's desire to fully recognize each employee's capability without resorting to an impossible-to-remember naming system, human resources (HR) should move away from taxonomy (classifying people) to "folksonomy" (tagging people).

In many organizations, we suspect that this is sometimes "tacitly" acknowledged – with people being allocated to projects based on a "gut feel" for their capabilities and suitability. But to tag them properly, the HR data system needs to be sophisticated enough to consolidate, calculate and report the available capability, FTE (full time equivalent) and head count (unique individuals) in the organization.

OFFER A DOUBLE CAREER PATH

Finally, as we have already suggested, it is important to offer people the possibility of a creative career choice: one that offers the chance to become a maestro or a virtuoso. Under existing educational programmes, all designers and researchers are trained in a specific capability: they are trained to be virtuosos. (As we write, we are unaware of any course offering training as a maestro. But if there is one, let us know: we would like to take part in it.)

That's why we believe you should offer, at a certain level of seniority on the virtuoso career path, a choice: develop into a maestro, or continue with specialist education and become an even more talented virtuoso. Then, for those able to choose either path, you should create the projects and special assignments that will enable them to practice the role they have selected.

14
Commitment 14: Nurture Your Talent

In his book *Open Innovation*, Henry Chesbrough promoted a new model for innovation, one that called for sharing and trading resources, IP and know-how in a bid to innovate together. We would now like to suggest applying these ideas to the issue of cultivating talent in people by proposing an "open talent management". This would entail cultivating young talent by sharing responsibilities, introducing cumulative or mass talent management and exchanging talent throughout the design community.

We've known companies that have continually encountered problems in finding the right talents in the maestro and virtuoso areas; especially the maestros, who are knowledgeable about full touchpoints, brands, people foresights and insights, as well as capable of orchestrating a brand experience. Now, unless those companies were totally blind and looking for people in completely the wrong way, we are forced to conclude that there are currently few people educated and experienced enough in the design profession to perform the role of maestro.

One of the reasons for such scarcity is the current education programme. As we've already said, we don't believe it fulfils the requirements for educating people to become maestros and, as far as we know, there are currently no courses that focus on creating a professional maestro capable of creatively directing the full brand experience across all touchpoints.

A MUSICAL ANALOGY

This all seems rather strange when you compare it with musical education. Although there are a number of successful conductors in the world who were trained to play an instrument (for example, Yutaka Sado was trained as a flautist and recently conducted the Berlin Philharmonic), we think we are right in saying that most conductors are people who trained to be a conductor. If this is so then why, in the design field, do we not train people to become maestros?

Universität für Musik und darstellende Kunst Wien (University of Music and Performing Arts Vienna) is one of several well-known universities with a long tradition of training conductors. Many conductors known and respected in the world of music today graduated from it: for example, Herbert von Karajan and Claudio Abbado. Its description of its conductor programme states that:

> The goal of the orchestral conducting degree is to educate conductors who recognize all the artistic and historical components of a piece of music. Furthermore, they must master conducting techniques well enough to convey information clearly to the ensemble and fulfil their responsibility to the composer.

Don't we have exactly same requirements for a maestro of design? We think so. We think we need a maestro who recognizes all the artistic (look and feel) and brand or propositional components of a brand experience. We think we also need a maestro who can master conducting techniques well enough to convey clearly information (about brand values, beliefs and unique propositions). And by

studying how the music world has been able to educate and
nurture a number of talented conductors, we are convinced
that design not only needs to learn from that example but
also to take action now.

INVEST IN THE FUTURE

Assuming you agree with what we've said here so far, then we
would go further and say it is essential for all senior design
leaders to take the initiative and invest their time in building
our (not mine and yours but our) future talent for the design
community. We need to install a policy of open talent management, a policy that will nurture scarce talent for our entire
design community. And we need to realize that this goes far
beyond talent management for our own organizations.

It's important to realize that this will *not* resolve any
problems you have with your current vacancy list –
especially if you need someone with enough experience in
the profession to pick up a mouse and finish a drawing as a
looming deadline approaches. What we are talking about is
a long-term investment for all of us in design, one that could
resolve all our talent and resource problems in the future.

The one and only asset of design is people. Therefore
investing in the education of future talent seems logical if
we all believe that design thinking and capability can contribute to the long-term happiness of all people. That's why
we really need to take action together to nurture upcoming
talents. So, in the rest of this chapter, we would like to share
our thinking about how to install open talent management
and to do so by focusing on the maestro capability.

A PROPOSAL

There are two essential groups of stakeholders in open talent
management. One is design schools. If we are to manage talent openly we need a more comprehensive and structural

partnership with design schools, one that combines such activities as setting assignments, sponsorship, student placements and internships. Therefore it's important to find a design school that can share our vision and beliefs and participate in the creation of the necessary programmes and lectures. By fully participating in – and sharing responsibility with design schools for – the creation of programmes and lectures, we can together produce comprehensive programmes that take place both in and out of the design school.

The other essential group consists of the senior leaders currently performing the maestro role in the design business. It would be good to have representatives of these leaders from a wide mix of fields (various categories of industries and agencies) to help offer young talent a wider perspective.

Working with design schools and senior design leaders, we believe we could create a unique educational training programme: one based in the theoretical world of a school but practiced in the reality of today's design world.

Therefore – assuming we could count on the participation of these two essential stakeholders – we would like to propose the creation of an educational "programme" in which they both collaborate.

PROGRAMME REQUIREMENTS

We would open the programme to people who have already graduated from one specific field of design capability. This will ensure that they possess basic design skills and have (probably) also gained some experience in one capability or another. We would make selections based on portfolios and interviews and, possibly, a workshop assignment designed to demonstrate the candidate's approach to a problem (since we believe that personality is another key factor and one that plays a big role in becoming a successful maestro).

First step
We would utilize several existing courses at the school we collaborate with. First year students should take courses in various capabilities – graphics, products, interaction and so on – to increase their understanding of each capability and strength.

Second step
We would then, with the help of experts and senior leaders in different fields, create several different lectures and curricula. These would increase the students' understanding of: branding and propositions; experience; touchpoints; people's perceptions and insights; and effective communication.

Third step
We would follow this up by assigning students to work on the creation of a brand experience. We could construct a curriculum that would enable them to work on real assignments with other students from other fields: such as design (i.e. product design, user interface design and communication design), economics and engineering. The number of assignments could be linked to the actual day-to-day requirements of outside business partners.
(Note: a programme like this has been initiated at the Institute of Design at Stanford – the Stanford d. School. As they state in their manifesto, "Students and faculty in engineering, medicine, business, law, the humanities, sciences, and education find their way here to take on the world's messy problems together").

Fourth step
Internship would enable students to work, as a junior Creative Director, in the real organization of each senior leader. This would help them build experience in real day-to-day situations. Such an internship programme should cover not only work assignments but also people management skills, financial skills, planning skills and so on.

We are not suggesting that each step takes one year; some of them could happen in parallel. Nor do we yet know how many years the programme would need to last. But since any school education must come to an end at some point, then perhaps when these students have understood the basics they should move out into the real world to increase their experience.

BUILD NETWORKS, EXTEND CAPABILITIES

Nurturing design (maestro) talent isn't the whole story however. You also always need to extend your capabilities. And, as far as design is concerned, the first step in doing that is to create and build a wide network of experts, partners, opinion leaders, consultants, universities and NGOs (and other such bodies and individuals) to form an extension of your team.

With such a network in place, you then need to give clear targets to your senior maestros and virtuosos, and expose both to their own competence networks through open forums, conferences and seminars and exhibitions. This not only helps motivate them, but also provides the opportunity for self-reflection and the chance to "cross-check" their competence by networking with people outside their office. It's also a good idea to involve some of your contacts in co-creation activities (see Chapter 3) within your projects by collaborating with opinion leaders, universities, NGOs and so on.

Your new network will help you discover some new expertise that complements your design capabilities. To integrate them further with other capabilities you may sometimes need to make them part of the team and nurture them internally. For example, when we were at Philips Design, we used an engineer who could make prototypes quickly and a people researcher who could facilitate – and lead – people-focused research. Why did we make them part of our team instead of simply creating a good partnership with external experts?

On one such project, the design team encountered problems translating our designers' visions into demonstrators because all the engineers the team partnered with from outside the design team couldn't get used to making models without a detailed technical specification. Although they were all excellent engineers, what the team needed were people who could translate (by working together) a design vision and language into a technical specification: it needed an internal "creative engineer" – someone who could work in both design and engineering. (At the time of writing, we have just encountered an associate of the Design Council who coaches engineers to become more creative in a programme sponsored by the RSA – Royal Society for the Arts.)

It was the same for the people researchers. We needed researchers who were fully aware of design requirements and language, who understood the design process and could therefore make their output fit smoothly and fully into the design process. It is essential that they are focused on the fact that the output of their research is input for – and focused on – achieving the best solutions.

To conclude, we would suggest that if you want to expand your design expertise further, you should devote some thought to the creation of an external network. When you want to maximize the benefits of expanding your expertise, it is a good idea to internalize all the new knowledge you gain by integrating it fully into your entire design process.

AN APPEAL

We genuinely believe in open talent management. We think such a programme would provide a much needed stimulus to producing more design maestros, and we are dedicated to making it a reality and looking for partners to work together on it. We believe we all should take responsibility for leading students in the right direction, not just for the future of design, but also for the future of people every-where.

And this is why we would ask anyone reading who shares our views and agrees with our suggested approach, to get in touch with us. We would very much like to collaborate with you.

You can contact us at the following address:
brand.romance.highdesign@gmail.com

15
Commitment 15: Create a Shared Culture

In Chapter 13, we pointed out the importance of clear descriptions for each role. That said, we believe there is something even more important: the creation of a shared culture.

THE POWER OF A SHARED CULTURE

In *Leading at a Higher Level* (2009), Demarest, Edmonds and Glaser write that, "Culture consists of the values, attitudes, beliefs, behaviours, and practices of the organizational members." That is why you, as a brand and a company, should create one culture based on your brand values and beliefs. The results of a team of people who have fully interiorized your brand values and beliefs, and who are all acting under one culture to create meaningful and relevant brand experience will be extremely powerful. The power of one shared culture will go far, far beyond the setting of policies, guidelines, KPIs and balanced score cards!

In their book, *Built to Last*, James Collins and Jerry Porras write that you should "strengthen your company by creating a cult-like culture." They continue:

> The point is to build an organisation that fervently preserves its core ideology in specific, concrete ways.

The visionary companies translate their ideologies into tangible mechanisms aligned to send a consistent set of reinforcing signals. They indoctrinate people, impose tightness of fit, and create a sense of belonging to something special through practical, concrete items.

BRINGING YOUR BRAND TO LIFE

So the question that follows is: can you shape the culture so that your design team shares an understanding of what is, and is not, the right brand experience? We believe you can. We believe you create a community able to "culturally judge" the direction of the brand experience without the need for any "rule books". In our experience, rule books are useless for describing the nuances, feelings and emotions of your brand; brands and companies that rely on rule books tend to see their brand identity as a grid and a template – something tangible, but also something lacking any emotion. They see it as separate from, and often different to, the culture of the organization.

Yet we believe it is only when you are able to create a shared culture that recognizes what is – or is not – in your brand experience, that you will also be able to bring your brand to life. This is because the cultural judgement we refer to here evolves over time, just as a language evolves and develops.

Consider the language you use today and the language people used in the past. They're not the same. Every year, every month, every day, peoples and societies introduce new habits and fashions in the way they speak. They invent new applications for words and new words entirely. Some of these new elements may be accepted by the whole culture and become a standard way of speaking for everyone, while others may be rejected and die out of use. The evolution of a language is not something controlled by a governmental rule book, but by the society – and the culture – that owns and uses it.

It is our firm belief that a design team can also create one such cultural community and society. They can create it under one brand and go beyond any rule books and guidelines to judge what is, and is not, part of your brand's creative direction.

Case Study – White Logistics

Haulage and storage is a difficult industry to turn a profit in, operating costs are increasing, it's fiercely competitive and as new technology helps with efficiencies, it also ushers in commoditization, leaving fewer opportunities to add value.

White Logistics & Storage is one of many in this industry. It's UK-based, owner-managed, with a staff of 85, a fleet of around 50 vehicles and a turnover of just over £6m (2010). Turnover had become stagnant and, although the balance-sheet was strong, its owner and MD, Judith Stracey, had been thinking about how to stem the losses from previous years and return to growth.

On the suggestion from the local business support service, Judith agreed to a meeting with Ellis Pitt, a design associate from the Design Council's Design Leadership Programme.

Judith readily admitted that she knew little about design and was initially sceptical. "Design, what's that got to do with us?" she admitted. "I thought design was just about putting the logo onto our lorries", she said at their initial meeting. However Ellis Pitt quickly changed her mind. He explained:

When I first met Judith, I wasn't sure I'd done a very good job of explaining what she would be saying "yes" or "no" to. Profit from groupage activity is won and lost in both the black art of planning, and thinking on your feet when things don't go according to plan. Notwithstanding technology, it's still largely a people business and a pressured environment working around the clock. A chance to think strategically and what design could bring to a business like this are the poor-relation to the business of the day.

...

But it was something I said about the drivers being a key brand touch-point, which resonated with Judith and that, coupled with her open mindedness, seemed to be enough to get a "yes, in principle".

Identifying opportunities

Pitt worked with a small team of multidisciplinary designers and the company's management to identify opportunities for design to influence the performance of the business. Their approach highlighted a number of opportunities including strategic planning, branding and communications and new services to drive growth. Ellis said:

Although it didn't feature prominently in the feedback at the end of the day, we were struck by the raft of stories in which deliveries had made it to their customers, sometimes against the odds. Brands are made of stories and the White's story was not being told well enough to influence the external perception of the business, position it in such a way that it "stands out from the crowd" in a very competitive marketplace and ensure recognition and "memorability" when potential customers are making decisions about which logistics company to use.

The design team got the sense that White's wasn't close enough to its customers and users to gain real insights into their habits and preferences. Doing so would give them advantages over their competitors.

The team also remarked on a number of occasions that although the culture of White's suggested there was good reason to be proud of what they do, with a "can do" attitude towards solving customers' problems, the staff didn't all share a sense of belonging, especially the drivers scattered to the four winds. Judith explained:

> As soon as talk touched on the potential for our drivers' behaviour to impact on the business, something that has always bothered me because in some respects it was beyond my control, I had a change of heart.
>
> ...
>
> We didn't think at that point we needed to think about our brand, though naive, we were open minded.

Led by Ellis, the management team prioritized the opportunities the team had identified. Many smaller, internal improvement projects were carried out but a decision was made to invest in three significant design projects:

1. To clearly define and agree a future ambition for the business and the operational decisions which would support it.

2. To strengthen the company's approach to brand and communications.

3. A service design project to harness insights about customers as a way of driving the introduction of new, value-adding, services.

The approach taken to these projects, however, had a significant impact on culture.

Design influencing culture

Brand and service designers worked together, with staff, in visits to talk to customers. Those insights were shared openly with all those in customer-facing roles at White's. The brand designers set about a solution that would capitalize on all that was working well at White's and use insights from talking to customers to leverage both internal and external communications. The Whites logistics service team, without knowing it, were already being inducted into the new brand.

Concurrent internal workshops brought cross-sections of staff together in ways they'd never done before; drivers saw things differently from credit-control staff, warehousing had suggestions for improving administration, directors listened and learned and designers absorbed.

As a priority for the service design team, an opportunity was scoped in a project nick-named "Knights of the Road", to train the drivers to become ambassadors of the White's new brand. Customers, suppliers and the general public see more of the drivers than anyone else in the company and as a brand "touch-point" they influence the perception of the company considerably. This now forms the induction and continual professional development of all drivers, existing and new.

The brand designers encapsulated the business's strengths in the phrase "Problem? Solved!" This provided the theme for the re-branding.

A spare meeting room was requisitioned, close to the heart of the business, (above the drivers' common room and adjacent to their training-room), to serve as a "war room". Meetings and workshops were held there using the walls as a place to post findings, notes, photos and design work. Every one of the staff members went there regularly to see what was going on and to add their own comments.

A short introduction to brainstorming in one of the Design Council's own workshops for participating companies took root in operations director Daniel Holland's mind and before they knew it a small group was using the wall of a smoking shelter, during tea-breaks, to figure-out ways to improve the allocation of pallets to vehicles. With a little light-touch guidance from the Design Council they used video and process-mapping techniques to review how it was being done and then started to redesign the process to reduce errors and delays and anticipate an increase in volume. They tried a few ideas out in the yard, in real-time, fine-tuning the things that worked and rejecting the ideas that didn't. The visibility of this helped create a momentum that's taken root in other areas of the business, with Daniel facilitating short, sharp sessions focused on improving the way they do things.

Judith has gone "on the record" a number of times since, perhaps the most significant testament to the work is her comment that:

What's been the most valuable about our experience of the Design Leadership Programme has been how our culture has changed; we now think far more strategically as a direct result.

In the midst of the recession, performance has improved. £500k of new business in the first nine months after launching the new White's brand and three years on, turnover has reached £6.435m. Recognition from the design industry has also been a real morale-booster for all involved. White's have won the following awards:

- Best of Show at the Design Week Awards 2012
- Best Identity at the Design Week Awards 2012
- D&AD Annual 2012 "In-book" status
- Identity chosen for publication in the "Creative Review Annual" 2012
- "Best Rebrand" at the Marketing Design Awards 2012
- "Best Corporate Rebrand" at the Transform Awards 2012.

White's are solving both their customers' problems and now some of their own, using design thinking to do so.

HEART OF YOUR ORGANIZATION

Creating a shared culture begins with your design team and their brand values and beliefs. If you imagine that your designers are the heart of your organization (see Figure 15.1), then we believe they must possess four key components to function fully and effectively.

Immerse

The values and beliefs of your design team should also, obviously, be based on your brand values and beliefs. Your community should be fully immersed in, and continuously embrace, your brand values and beliefs to develop an almost "cult-like" culture. (See the immerse your employees section.)

Share

Every daily discovery by every individual should be shared by everyone in your company, in dialogues between both groups and individuals. (See the share and stimulate section.)

Create

Each day, each member of your team should face once constant challenge: how do I create? They must always try to find ways to offer relevant and meaningful solutions by delivering a total brand experience to your end-users and customers. (See the find ways to create section.)

Discover

By working on everyday challenges, every member of the team will discover something new almost daily. Such discoveries can be the result not only of your own work, but also from networking with external individuals and events. (See the discover something new section.)

Figure 15.1 *The heart of your organization*

IMMERSE YOUR EMPLOYEES

If you are to have one shared culture, then all your employees must completely immerse themselves in your brand values and beliefs.

Most companies and brands manifest their brand values and beliefs in their internal documents and publications. Many brands boast nice "coffee table" documents that articulate their values and beliefs with a set of texts and supporting photographs, while others use websites with a mix of text and short film clips. Philips, whom we worked for, offered a value and belief statement; a glossy brand book (and an A4-sized concise version); a pocket-sized reference brochure; a website; and, from time to time, short films about its brand. By utilizing all these materials in our design group we organized a number of regular interaction sessions for people so that they could immerse themselves in the brand values and beliefs.

All this was – and is – very effective. Yet we also know of something far more effective and powerful when it comes to immersing all your employees in your brand values and beliefs. In Chapter 2 we touched on the importance of helping internal groups to understand what people desire, and find relevant and meaningful, by creating long-term exploration projects. As we mentioned in Chapter 2, the idea for this is based on what neuroscientists David Ingvar and William Calvin have called "memories of the future".

A multi-purpose event

We believe that actually thinking about potential future developments for your brand will open your employees' minds to new possibilities and make your brand values and beliefs tangible to them. In Chapter 12 we described Yasushi's experiences working on Philips's Simplicity Event. For those events, the brand experience of future concepts was created with the aid of experience demonstrators: designed and staged "snapshots" of real life environments in which the concepts might operate. This helped visitors at the event to easily immerse themselves in, and absorb, the story for each concept.

Obviously the main target audience was external stakeholders, but each event was also highly valued by the company's internal employees. Yasushi was told personally – and read in the feedback loops – that the event had finally helped them understand what the brand stood for and what it was trying to achieve. For them it was strategy made real. It wasn't a series of PowerPoint slides crammed with drawings and bullet points: it was something tangible. And of all the events in that company's HR programme, the employees always placed The Simplicity Event at the top.

So if you are looking for ways to effectively communicate your brand values and beliefs to your employees, we would say don't spend too much of your resources on booklets and films. Create multi-purpose events that illustrate the future concepts of your brand story instead.

SHARE AND STIMULATE

To enable, and stimulate, "sharing" in your culture, there are a number activities and programmes you can instigate. For example, you could share and discuss brand values and beliefs; exchange your multi-purpose expertise and High Design approaches; share and discuss cutting-edge knowledge and newly developed competencies; or share and immerse your designers in relevant and meaningful design articulation through creative direction. We are sure that if your designers were to develop new programmes based on these topics, it would be the embryo of a new culture for them all.

The contents of these programmes should come from each team member's everyday challenges and achievements. All you need to do is install a central organization that will set up an annual programme based on newly-discovered content filtered by company strategy and the latest developments in your brand. In our experience, such programmes are perceived not only as "cultural creation" but also as the "oxygen" needed to stimulate creativity and provide energy for their day-to-day responsibilities and work.

Finally, if you want to discover new contents for such a programme, you can use the quality review process (see Chapter 11 for more about this). Installing such a process will enable senior management to "discover" the embryo(s) of new culture(s) in your team that you may want to grow and evolve.

SHARE CREATION TO DISCOVER TOGETHER

Besides the day-to-day individual challenges of creation, you can also help to create one culture by taking up challenges to resolve shared social concerns. Rather than discuss this in abstract terms, we would like to offer a practical example of a programme Yasushi was once involved in at Philips. It was called Philanthropy by Design and was initiated and lead by Stefano Marzano.

> Philanthropy by Design is about harnessing our creativity for humanitarian causes and sustainable development. We are fortunate enough to be in a position where we can help as a company, and we are proud that our activities can have such broad positive impact on people's lives.
>
> Stefano Marzano, founder of Philanthropy by
> Design, 2011

Philanthropy by Design's aim was to create and deploy humanitarian propositions that would address social and environmental issues affecting the more fragile groups in our societies. It was a programme that used design talent to develop meaningful and sustainable solutions that could contribute to a better future for all. It also helped to open up new perspectives in co-creating value through cooperation with "unconventional" partners such as aid organizations, public bodies and social players who could offer complementary expertise and values.

As a part of this cultural programme Yasushi and his team organized an event entitled A Sustainable Design Vision, with approximately 275 designers from all over world. It took place in 2005 in Eindhoven, in the Netherlands and was attended not only by designers but also by some of the world's foremost sustainability thinkers and practitioners (including representatives from such leading NGOs as Save the Children and Médecins Sans Frontières). The team started the event by sharing – with the help of external stakeholders – insights into the quality of life in the most fragile categories of our society.

(If you would like to find out more about the approach Philips Design took in Philanthropy by Design, see Rocchi and Kusume's "Empowering Creativity", in Kandachar and Halme, *Sustainability Challenges and Solutions at the base of the Pyramid.*)

CREATE, DISCOVER AND SHARE

What came out of the Philanthropy by Design event were several promising concepts that the team was able to develop further with designers and respective external stakeholders. One involved improved efficiency and quality control of, as well as simplified training for, the early detection of malaria and pneumonia. Another looked at safer and healthier cooking indoors, which then became the first actual project launched. It was called the Chulha and you can find out more at: http://www.lowsmoke-chulha.com.

However the key point we would like to stress here is not the success of the Philanthropy by Design programme. What we want to stress is that to create a shared culture, it is important that you share some social concerns with your team and that you base your contribution on your brand values and beliefs – to make it, if you like, part of your "brand citizenship". You must give your team the opportunity to think beyond your brand's daily business so that it can make a contribution to society based on your brand values and beliefs (*immerse*). You must give it the chance to *create, discover* and *share*.

If you do this, you will offer your designers an opportunity to embrace your brand values and beliefs further. At the same time you will also provide them with the motivation and satisfaction that comes from using their capabilities to contribute directly to society. You will bring a level of engagement and understanding to your colleagues that will enrich your whole brand culture.

Conclusion

We hope, now you've reached the end of the book, that you understand why we believe the High Design principle is the formula you need to build a truly loved brand with your audience. Because it treats end-users and customers with love; and because it creates direct, holistic brand design experiences for all end-users and customers.

What we'd like to offer in this final chapter is a summary – a check list, if you will – of the High Design principles, and of the 15 commitments you need to build a loving relationship with your audience. We would like to conclude with an actual example of High Design in action.

THE FOUR PRINCIPLES OF HIGH DESIGN

High Design is people-focused

- To love your audiences, you must know them – everything from their future needs to their current wants. This is your starting point.

- To understand your audiences, you must decode their mechanisms of experience (the five steps of engagement).

- To fulfil the un-met wishes of your audience you must explore their ideal experiences.

- To continuously satisfy your audience, you need to continuously innovate. To continuously innovate, and develop further together, you need to share your brand vision of the future and receive feedback from people and society.

High Design is business-integrated

- To authentically communicate your brand values and beliefs to your audience, you must think of your brand as a person and make sure you present a clear and consistent personality – behaving and appearing in an appropriate manner supported by a brand design architecture.

- To maximize the value of design thinking and capability in the business creation process, apply three simple, focused activities to make your own design process.

- To maximize the power of cross-functional teams, apply design thinking and capability to build a shared vocabulary so you can then create holistic brand experiences of meaningful and relevant propositions.

High Design is research-based

- To learn about your audience, involve them by creating a community. Co-creation makes your dreams come true: you can be emotionally engaged with your loved ones 24 hours a day, 365 days a year!

- To receive appropriate feedback from your audience, ask them relevant questions.

- To keep your finger on your audiences' pulse, search for and build measurements that can be applied as your "love meter", so you can then measure design's contribution to building a loved brand.

High Design is multidisciplinary

- To orchestrate a brand experience, install a maestro to conduct it and a number of virtuosi to produce the required performance.

- To orchestrate one brand experience, don't only rely on a rule book. Build a shared culture centred on understanding your brand.

- To sustain the future talent of your brand, share responsibility by installing open talent management. Do not limit your perspective with short-term issues.

THE 15 COMMITMENTS YOU NEED TO BUILD A LOVED BRAND

We have written this book to show how companies can build a loved brand with their audiences, and to describe the 15 commitments required to do so. Some are easier to implement than others. Some require long-term planning. All demand long-term commitment. Here is a summary of each of them.

Commitment 1: Think of your brand as a person

To authentically communicate your brand values and beliefs to your audiences, you must think of them as a person – with their own values and beliefs – and make sure that a clear and consistent personality is always presented.

Commitment 2: Understand current and future needs

If you truly love your audiences, you will not only think about their short-term, but also anticipate their long-term happiness. To continuously satisfy your audiences, you need to continuously innovate to fulfil their needs, sometimes even before they are aware of them. This is essential for a brand's long-term sustainability.

Commitment 3: Co-create with people

To really understand and learn about your audiences, you should involve them in your mission by creating a community. "Co-creation" involves the creation of "a permanent emotional engagement with your audiences". It does not mean involving people in only one phase of your business or product creation process. Co-creation enables you to change from being a "receiver and observer" of insights – someone who purchases anonymous data or only observes an audience without interacting with it – to a "leader and stimulator" – someone who generates insights that not only apply to a design and business approach but also truly inspire all cross-function teams.

Commitment 4: Understand people's "experience"

To learn about your audiences, you must also explore and define their ideal experiences. But first you must decode their mechanisms of experience through the five stages of experience (imagination, impression, discovery, use and memory).

Commitment 5: Measure and optimize

To continuously monitor the effectiveness of your ability to fulfil the needs of your audience, you need to measure and optimize what you do on a constant basis. You should always determine the key function and achievements you want from the particular touchpoint, based on its role in your loved one's experience or "journey". Then ensure you are asking the right questions. Finally, make sure you optimize and build your knowledge over a number of years – to ensure that your long-term relationship retains and builds its memory.

Commitment 6: Introduce a "love tester"

To check that your audiences still fully appreciate you, you should monitor their reactions regularly. Make sure you use the right measurements for your purpose and use them constantly so that you will always have tangible results when reviewing, monitoring and improving your performance.

Commitment 7: Build a brand design architecture

If you want to behave – and appear – in a particular way towards your audiences at all times across touchpoints, time and space, you will need an organizing structure: a brand design architecture. This will help you "orchestrate" your brand experience across your company portfolio by enabling you to look through the eyes of your audiences. It will help you apply an "outside-in" approach.

Commitment 8: Continuously innovate

A brand needs to innovate – and keep innovating – to ensure and maintain its long-term sustainability. Therefore if you want to continue to meet the changing needs and wishes of your audience, you must constantly explore and anticipate those needs. Only by having a clear vision of how to contribute to the future happiness and prosperity of people and society will your brand become a trusted leader in its field.

Commitment 9: Give your value proposition the four design drivers

To fulfil the needs of your audiences in a coherent and meaningful fashion, your value proposition must be driven by consistent underlying principles. In this book, these are known as the four design drivers: meaningful, distinctive, attractive and coherent. They are vital to planning the scope of your propositions, to maximizing their value to your audiences and therefore your brand.

Commitment 10: Define your brand expression

An audience experiences your brand through its touch-points. Therefore the design of these touchpoints has the potential to differentiate and create a specific identity that provides instant recognition for, and access to, the brand values and beliefs. Whatever approach you take to your identity (brand expression), it must be an authentic expression of your brand values and beliefs, as well as one that is both meaningful and relevant to your audiences.

Commitment 11: Embrace three design principles

If you truly love and care about your audiences, you can take three simple steps to fulfil their desires: 1) you must understand your audiences and their needs and wants; 2) you must explore what will fulfil those needs and desires; and 3) you must create the products and services that meet those needs, and the way they are experienced.

Commitment 12: Create one vocabulary for the whole organization

To meet the needs of your audiences, the people behind your brand must work in a fully integrated, outside-in manner. To make this happen, you must ensure that all parts of the organization are working towards common goals through a common vocabulary. To do this, use the tools and skills of design to translate topics into tangible forms during the stages of the business creation process. Use design to play an integrator's role with all stakeholders (both inside and outside the company).

Commitment 13: Recognize the maestro and the virtuoso

To ensure that the people in your design team collaborate seamlessly – especially if your organization is large, complex and covers many territories – you must identify and install the two leadership roles essential for the orchestration of a brand experience: the maestro and the virtuoso.

Commitment 14: Nurture your talent

The one and only asset of design is people and in order to build a team that is truly dedicated to your audience you must nurture your talent by sharing responsibilities, introducing cumulative or mass talent management and exchanging skills throughout your design community. It also helps to extend your capabilities beyond your organization – as well as beyond conventional design capabilities – to create and build a wide network of experts, partners, opinion leaders, consultants, universities and NGOs (and other such bodies and individuals) as an extension of your team.

Commitment 15: Create a shared culture

You need to shape the culture of your company so that your design team shares an understanding of what is, and is not, the right brand experience for your audiences. It needs to be able to "culturally judge" the direction of the brand experience without the need for any rule books because, in reality, rule books are useless for describing the nuances, feelings and emotions of your brand, which can be quite separate and often different from the culture of the organization.

Acknowledgements

We would like to take this opportunity to thank all the people who have worked with us during our careers. All those who creatively inspired us every day sparked the creation of building a truly loved brand and all the High Design commitments. We would especially like to thank:

Stefano Marzano
Stefano is the father of the High Design philosophy, a number of thoughts in this book and the one who also educated us, Yasushi and Neil, in it. Although we started working with him much earlier, we really began to collaborate in 1999 with our work on brand design. He is the most creative, charismatic manager and leader of people we have met in our careers and we both deeply admire his work, his thinking and his creativity.

Mark Churchman
Mark, one of the most respected creative directors we have ever met, is able to describe very emotional issues in rational and structural terms and has worked closely with Yasushi on all branding and creative direction issues. Many of the ideas, thoughts and topics in this book – such as "Design ensures that a brand makes the right emotional connection with its audience" – came from him.

Joanna Crawshaw and **Claire Dorel-Watson**
Jo and Claire are two key players who worked on several brand design programmes and are also the owners of a

number of thoughts, ideas and topics in this book. Jo is creative, highly structured and able to clarify when clarity is needed. She is a fantastic partner for the times when the intangible needs to become tangible. Claire is just as creative and inspirational, always goes the extra mile and never gives up! Without their contributions, several ideas in this book would never have emerged.

Bas Griffioen and **Annemieke Strous**
Bas is a senior programme and project manager, one who possesses not only the patience but also the stamina to take difficult requests and realize them constructively. He is also the man who, in conjunction with Annemieke, was behind many Design awards. It was their structured management that established the network we needed to build our insights.

Thomas Marzano
Thomas is a young and talented creative director, and the intellectual leader when it came to communication design and digital issues at Philips Design. Several ideas in this book came from his work on co-creation and full touch points. Yasushi especially learned a lot from him about the new digital environment – although he cannot claim to be one of his most accomplished students.

Reon Brand and **Simona Rocchi**
Reon was a teacher in all foresight and socio-cultural issues. He is not only an excellent planner, but also possesses the ability to realize and deliver to strict deadlines. Simona was one of the leading thinkers on sustainability issues and the leader of Philips's Philanthropy by Design activities. Without her leadership, Yasushi would never have managed the number of achievements this programme can claim. The idea of co-innovation came from Reon and Simona's work.

Marion Verbucken and **Bertrand Rigot**
Marion and Bertrand are two of the most talented creative directors we have ever worked with. They are both extremely creative and passionately committed to their work. They led all the Next Simplicity projects between 2005 and 2008. The idea that building a loved brand is actually the same process as building a loving relationship with a partner came from their work in Next Simplicity, 2005 (and is described in detail in the book that accompanied the event).

Mili Docamporama and **Claudia Lieshout**
Yasushi learned a lot by working closely with Mili and Claudia, on both people and trend research matters. Mili managed to establish and apply various people-focused tools in Philips while Claudia, clearly the leader in trend issues, established and installed a number of very helpful research tools.

Patrick Lerou and **Burcu Onar Konus**
Patrick and Burcu are the two market intelligence managers who helped Yasushi in the investigation and creation of the methodology required to utilize NPS data when evaluating design contribution. Patrick led the creation of the hypothesis of approach, while Burcu made it operational. Both of them were very proactive, committed to the challenge and knowledgeable about the subject. Without their involvement, Yasushi would never have gained the insights he did, nor created the methodology.

Paul Thursfield and **Gavin Proctor**
Paul and Gavin led the creative team in one of the annual innovation programmes in which Yasushi gained many insights into ways of co-creating with people and maximizing the value of using the customer journey. Paul has a

unique expertise of mixing product and interaction design, which in turn gives him the ability to think in terms of a full brand experience. Gavin is not only highly reliable, but also a committed, well-organized and multi-skilled manager capable of working on multiple aspects of any project simultaneously.

All those who worked at Philips Design from 1990 to 2012
We would also like to thank all those others – not mentioned in person – who in one way or another contributed to making the High Design philosophy fully operational in our daily work.

We also would like to acknowledge that the experience design thinking and phases (description of stages) were developed by Philips Design with many people involved such as Irene McWillam, John Cass, Lorna Goulden and Paul McGroary.

Nick Garlick
Nick helped turn Yasushi's Janglish (Japanese-English) into proper British English. Nick also helped both of us to put our story from an outside-in point of view.

Design Council
We would like to thank the Design Council for their support and endorsement and for the case studies and evidence provided from their own design leadership programme. In particular we'd like to say thanks to:

Mat Hunter
Mat is the Design Council Chief Design Officer and we would like to say thanks to Mat for his evaluation and input to the book and for providing advice and examples. His experience and endorsement has guided us to also target CEO's with this book and bring these principles to the

attention of the boardroom, not just the design and marketing departments.

Ellie Runcie
Ellie is the Design Council Director for the Design Leadership Programme and we would like to say thanks to Ellie for providing Neil with the opportunity to take his design experience to many UK start-ups, small and medium sized companies and universities through the Design Leadership Programme and for her support in providing input and examples from the programme.

Bibliography

Aaker, David, A. *Managing Brand Equity* (Free Press, 1991).

———. *Brand Leadership* (Free Press, 2000).

———. *Brand Portfolio Strategy* (Free Press, 2004).

Anderson, Chris. *Free* (Hyperion, 2009).

Ariely, Dan. *Predictably Irrational* (HarperCollins Publishers, 2008).

Baghai, Mehrdad, Coley, Stephen and White, David. *The Alchemy of Growth* (Perseus Publishing, 2000).

Bloomberg Businessweek. "Behind Philips' 'High Design'" (25 October, 2005).

Calvin, William, H. "How to Think What No One Has Ever Thought Before", in J. Brockman and K. Matson (eds) *How Things Are: A Science Tool-Kit for the Mind*, (William Morrow & Co, 1995), pp. 151–63.

Cattell, Heather, E. P. and Schuerger, James M. *Essentials of 16PF Assessment* (John Wiley & Sons, Inc., 2003).

Chesbrough, Henry. *Open Innovation – The New Imperative for Creating and Profiting from Technology* (Harvard Business Press, 2006).

Collins, Jim and Porras, Jerry. *Built to Last* (HarperBusiness Essentials, 1994).

Demarest, Garry, Edmonds, Chris and Glaser, Bob, "Managing a Successful Culture Transformation", in Ken Blanchard (ed.) *Leading at a Higher Level* (FT Press, 2009).

Design Council of London. Various case studies (available at: http://www.designcouncil.org.uk/leadership).

Design Council of London. "Value of Design Fact Finder Report" (accessed 21/06/2013, available at: http://www.designcouncil.org.uk/our-work/Insight/Research/How-businesses-use-design/Added-Value-2007/).

Design Council of London and SDL/The Research Business International. "What, Why and How of Branding" (2007).

Difference Between.net. "Difference Between Values and Beliefs". 21 May 2011 (accessed 21/06/2013, available at: http://www.differencebetween.net/language/difference-between-values-and-beliefs/).

Doblin. "The Ten Types of Innovation" (accessed 21/06/2013, available at: http://www.doblin.com/thinking/).

Eric. V. The beforemario blog (accessed 21/06/2013, available at: http://blog.beforemario.com).

Gladwell, Malcom. *Blink* (Crown Publishing Group, 2010).

Ind, Nicholas. *The Corporate Brand* (Macmillan Press, 1997).

Ingvar, D. H. "Memory of the Future: An Essay on the Temporal Organization of Conscious Awareness". *Human Neurobiology*, 1985, vol 4, pp. 127–36.

Johnson, Hugh. *How to Enjoy Your Wine* (Simon & Schuster, 1999).

Kahneman, Daniel. *Thinking Fast and Slow* (Penguin, 2012).

Kapferer, Jean-Noël. *Strategic Brand Management* (Kogan Page, 1997).

Karmayogi. "Behavior, Character, Personality". December 1977 (accessed 22/06/2013, available at: http://www.karmayogi.net/?q=behaviorcharacterpersonality).

Knapp, Duane, E. *The Brand Mindset* (McGraw-Hill, 2000).

Lickerman, Alex, M.D. "Happiness in this World: Personality vs. Character, The Key to Discerning Personality from Character". *Psychology Today*, 3 April, 2011.

Lindstrom, Martin. *Brand Sense* (Free Press, 2005).

——. *Buyology* (Random House, 2009).

——. *Brand Sense: Sensory Secrets Behind the Stuff We Buy* (Free Press, 2010).

Marzano, Stefano. *Creating Value by Design: Thoughts and Facts* (V+K Publishing, 1998).

——. "Flying over Las Vegas". Keynote speech at the 17th World Design Conference of the International Council of Societies (ICSID), Ljubljana, 1992.

——. "The Role of Design" (Philips Design, 1999).

——. "Aligning Management and Business towards Sustainable Development" (1999)

——. "Let us Begin". Keynote speech at IDSA conference in Monterray California, 2002.

——. "Design – Key Factor for Success". Keynote speech at German Marketing Association Conference Hamburg, 2004.

——. "A Question of Choice". Keynote speech at the 10th European International Design Management Conference, Amsterdam, 2006.

——. "Celebration time!". Keynote speech at the Philips Simplicity Event, London, 2006.

——. *Past Tense, Future Sense* (Bis Publishers 2006).

——. "Driving Innovation in Corporate Culture: How Design Supports the CEO Turning this Challenge into an Opportunity". Keynote speech at the CEO and Innovation Leadership seminar in Hong Kong, 2009.

——. "Designing the Future in a Changing Market". Keynote speech at the DMI Europe, Milan, 2009.

——. "Does Your Customer Love You?". (A few words with, 2011, accessed 28/06/2013, available at: http://www.design.philips.com/philips/sites/philipsdesign/

about/design/designnews/newvaluebydesign/january
2011/afewwordswith.page).

———. "Creative Culture: A New Humanism". Speech (date
and location unknown).

Mother's Service Society, The. "Manners-Behavior-
Character-Personality-Individuality" 23 May 2011
(accessed 21/06/2013, available at: http://www.dif-
ferencebetween.net/language/difference-between-
values-and-beliefs/#ixzz2Wvmq12gt).

Neumeier, Marty. *Brand Gap* (New Riders, 2006).

Oakland, J. *Total Quality Management* (Heinemann
Professional, 1989).

O'Neil, Dennis, Dr. Cultural Anthropology Tutorials website (accessed 22/06/2013, at: http://www.palomar.
edu/anthropology/).

Pine, Joseph and Gilmore, James. *The Experience
Economy* (Harvard Business Press, 1999).

Profit Impact of Market Strategy (PIMS). "Brand
Innovation 2000" study with assistance from IMD
for the European Brand Association (2000).

Reichheld, Fred. *The Ultimate Question* (Harvard Business
School Publishing Corporation, 2006).

Ries, Al and Ries, Laura. *The 22 Immutable Laws of
Branding* (HarperBusiness Essentials, 1998).

Rocchi, Simona and Kusume, Yasushi. "Empowering
Creativity", in Prabhu Kandachar and Minna Halme
(eds) *Sustainability Challenges and Solutions at the
Base of the Pyramid* (Greenleaf publishing, 2008).

Rocchi, Simona and Kusume, Yasushi. *Philanthropy by
Design* (Koninklijke Philips Electronics, 2011).

Royal Philips Electronics, "Next Simplicity" programme
2005, 2006 and 2007 (accessed 28/06/2013, available at:

http://www.youtube.com/watch?v=4lRlp61jMpY
http://www.youtube.com/watch?v=R-Cz144-qyQ&feature
=related

http://www.youtube.com/watch?v=TTHtMqHyU4w&feature=related

http://www.youtube.com/watch?v=6ZfIgdIgXDk&feature=related

http://www.youtube.com/watch?v=-adiqR9b-4o&feature=related

http://vimeo.com/8118794)

Sinek, Simon. *Start with Why* (Portfolio, 2009).

Wetzel, Gereon. EL BULLI Cooking in progress by Gereon Wetzel (Alive Mind, 2011).

Zec, Peter and Jacob, Burkhard. *Design Value* (Red Dot Publishing, 2010).

Index

References to figures are shown in *italics*.

Printed and bound in Great Britain by
CPI Group (UK) Ltd, Croydon, CR0 4YY